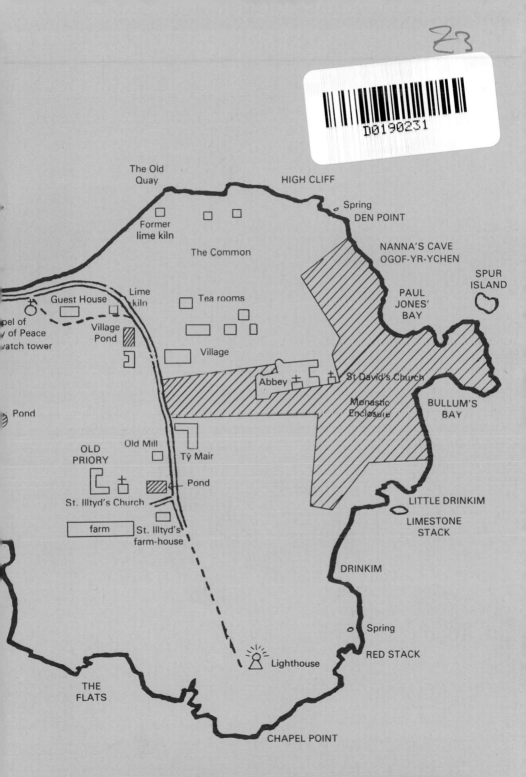

The Old Quay

HIGH CLIFF

Former lime kiln

Spring
DEN POINT

The Common

NANNA'S CAVE
OGOF-YR-YCHEN

SPUR ISLAND

Lime kiln

Tea rooms

Guest House

PAUL JONES' BAY

pel of
y of Peace
watch tower

Village Pond

Village

St David's Church

Abbey

Monastic Enclosure

BULLUM'S BAY

Pond

Old Mill

Old Priory

OLD PRIORY

Tŷ Mair

Pond

St. Illtyd's Church

LITTLE DRINKIM

LIMESTONE STACK

farm

St. Illtyd's farm-house

DRINKIM

Spring

RED STACK

Lighthouse

THE FLATS

CHAPEL POINT

Caldey

Caldey

Roscoe Howells

Gomer Press
1984

First Impression/March 1984

ISBN 0 86383 087 0

© Roscoe Howells

Printed by Gomer Press, Llandysul, Dyfed

To my many Caldey friends,
on the island and the mainland,
past, present and yet to be.

Contents

List of Illustrations

Foreword

by Professor Glanmor Williams, M.A., D. Litt.

Those who know Roscoe Howells or his books will not need me to tell them that he is one of that fast-diminishing breed, a genuine character. His writing, like his conversation, is the expression of a racy, energetic, humorous, distinctive individual. When they made him, they broke the mould. He says that in this book he wanted to write his own work in his own way; he seems to me to have succeeded—triumphantly and inimitably.

What a splendid subject he chose to write about this time! It's true that he's written about a number of Pembrokeshire islands before, and he's even told part of the story of Caldey in his book, *Total Community*. But this time he's given himself more elbow-room and told more of the story of the whole island and its people and not just about the monastery there. This is a narrative that has allowed all his talents as an author full play: the quick ear for a good story, the novelist's awareness of an interesting character, the poet's eye for nature's beauty, and the writer's pen to record it all in memorable fashion.

Though Caldey is a small island its history is rich, ancient, diversified and highly individual. Its main occupations have been farming, fishing, quarrying and, one must add, piety—though rarely of the long-faced and over-solemn kind. None of these has been without its hardship and failure as well as its success and recompense. Perhaps it was that very uncertainty, with the dividing-line between victory and disaster always finely-drawn, that has constituted its deep and appealing charm for generations of human beings.

Many of those who have lived there have been remarkable individuals whom Roscoe, with his sure sense and fluent pen, has vividly brought to life. Men like Cabot Kynaston or James Taylor Hawksley or Done Bushell or Aelred Carlyle, and families like the Webbs, the Thomases and the Banners. Communities old and new are all there: prehistoric people and modern seafarers, early Celtic saints and recent sinners, medieval monks and twentieth century devotees, shipwrecks and tourists, spring picnics and psychical research, agricultural workers and quarry labourers, farming folk and fishermen.

Roscoe seems to have devoured voraciously everything that has ever been written about Caldey and its history and, as often as not, he has his own down-to-earth comments to pass on the accuracy or common sense of what he's read. More than that, in so many instances he has himself known the people who were involved and has obviously engaged in long and sympathetic but probing conversations with them, designed to tease out the full details of their story.

I have had the good fortune to know Roscoe for many years and I greatly admire his books. Of all the ones I've read this is the one that has made the deepest impact on me. If Caldey has put Roscoe under its enduring spell, I am sure that he, in turn, will certainly enchant his readers.

Glanmor Williams

Acknowledgements

As always, this is, at one and the same time, both the most pleasant and the most difficult part of writing a book.

It is always pleasant to be able to offer thanks and acknowledge indebtedness. It is almost impossible, rather than merely difficult, to know where to draw the line when the number of those who have helped is so vast. Perhaps the dedication of the book will go some way to rectifying the many omissions which are inevitable.

Even so, there will always be those who must merit a special mention.

Firstly, of course, there is the Rt Rev Dom Robert O'Brien, to whom I am immensely indebted, not only for his personal friendship, but for the trust he showed in allowing me access to so many of the Community's private papers and records. Fr Stephen, the Procurator, was also, as always, most helpful and encouraging.

Having access to the late Fr Dominic's horde of pictures was of tremendous help, particularly in a work where I have tried to avoid using pictures which have been used previously, especially in *Total Community* and the second edition of *The Sounds Between*. To those from outside the Community who have made their precious family pictures available I am also greatly indebted, as well as to Mr Graham Hughes of Squibbs Studios for skilled work on various negatives.

Fr Robert, Fr Stephen and Fr David Williams were, in addition, extremely kind in reading the manuscript at various stages and making many helpful suggestions.

At Prinknash Abbey Dom Hildebrand was most helpful in answering many queries after searching through the archives there.

At the National Library of Wales I received, as always, marvellous help, especially from Mr Emrys Williams, the staff in the newspaper reading room, and, although he has long since retired, from Dr B. G. Charles who, understandably, is still drawn there as by a magnet.

Amongst the scholars, Major Francis Jones and Dr Fred Cowley were also most helpful.

From that tower of strength at the Pembrokeshire County Library, Mrs Joan Evans, I received the usual valuable help, as I did from all the staff there. At the Pembrokeshire Records Office I received a great deal of help from Messrs Jonathan Pepler and John Owen, which went far beyond the call of duty, and useful help was also forthcoming from the Carmarthen Records Office.

The two Superintendent Registrars in the county, Mr Lyn Jenkins at Haverfordwest and Mrs Margaret Rowlands at Pembroke, were marvellously patient in sorting out my innumerable enquiries. Nor, in this context, do I forget the vast knowledge which the late Mr Vincent Cunnick always made available to me before his untimely death.

I spent many hours at Tenby's splendid little museum where everybody concerned gave freely of their time and went to endless trouble on my behalf.

Many names have been mentioned in the course of this work, and from this it will be evident to how many people, on the island and on the mainland, I am greatly indebted. They include members of the large Cummins family as well as the host of others with less obvious Caldey connections.

The islanders, the boatmen, and the people of Tenby all know the extent of my indebtedness to them and I ask them now to accept my thanks.

To my wife, for typing the manuscript and contending, without too many complaints, with my execrable handwriting, I add such thanks as are due in addition to those which will be rather more obvious from the book itself.

Lastly, a special 'thank you' to Professor Glanmor Williams, not only for his ready willingness in agreeing to write the Foreword and his more than generous references, but for his many words of encouragement on various occasions over the years.

With so much help from so many scholars it is only necessary to conclude by stating the obvious, which is that the mistakes are all my own work.

R.H.

Chapter 1

A prayerful place and its setting

'Such then, is Caldey Island, richer it may be in its monastic memories than in the commercial activities of modern life, but whilst the human race is ruled, as it is and ever will be ruled, by sentiment, imagination and religion, whilst all that most enriches it is due to the efforts and the prayers of those who have passed behind the veil, such memories will still remain a power, none more effectual, to influence and mould our lives.'

Thus did the Rev William Done Bushell conclude the original edition of his little book, *Caldey: An Island of The Saints*, and it is appropriate to quote from such a source because history will show that his own coming to Caldey had a great bearing, both directly and indirectly, on the story of the island's inhabitants for many years to come.

Caldey is, then, a prayerful place. It is a place of great spirituality. But, whilst this is always evident, it is not always recognised. It is one thing for Caldey to be seen as quiet, or peaceful, or restful, or different, or a place apart. It is something else to be recognised for what it is as a result of men having given their lives there to God in prayer for years beyond number.

It takes time for such a spiritual atmosphere to build up, and no doubt it takes something else again for any particular person to respond to it. It is bound to be something more than imagination, for example, that causes just about everybody who comes into our chapel in Amroth to remark on the feeling of warmth and friendship. I was especially conscious of this tremendous feeling of prayerfulness a few years ago in the Catholic church at Dingle on the west coast of Ireland, and this is understandable when it is remembered that people have prayed there since time out of mind for loved ones putting out from this little fishing place.

About half-a-century ago Geoffrey Hoare wrote in his book, *Caldey, An Isle of the Severn Sea*, 'In view of the many articles (some true, others quite the reverse) that have appeared from time to

1

The Calvary, given by Mrs Fflorens Roach

'Wanderer stay still and think
On me here a little while
How I hung on the cross, so
That thou shouldst come to me.'

G. G. *Hoare*

time in our excitable press, it is perhaps a thankless task to write of an island as well known as Caldey.

Yet during my many visits I have often felt the need of a book which would, with the addition of a little romance, tend to make the island a closer acquaintance.'

Therein lies the problem, for the author then went on to record what he admitted were his own 'liberal-minded impressions', and to some extent detracted from the value of what was a useful book. In any case, there was no need for him to add a little romance, for it is there on Caldey to full measure and overflowing. He was young at the time anyway.

In her book *Bardsey, Gate of heaven*, Catherine Daniel said, 'It is a feature of romanticism to seek the things of God without God. To our forefathers, it would have been vanity to gaze upon the beauties of nature with the eyes of a soul not reconciled by penance with the entire order of God. That is one difference between the old world and the new.'

What I Ioare said about our excitable press is only too true, and it is incredible to find, not only how many inaccuracies have been written about Caldey over the years, but to realise that they are still being written. Even those writers who are not necessarily looking for effect have so often been content to go to secondary sources, and those sources are themselves sometimes in error. On the other hand, much which has been written is extremely good. Unfortunately, the better informed writers have never tackled the story in one good book, so that to learn the whole story it is necessary to seek a little here and a little there.

New evidence, of course, will always come to light, to make more plain what was previously obscure, or to make nonsense of accepted theories. What I hope to do is to put the record straight, as far as I am competent to do so, by sorting out the best that has so far been offered, from that which can more obviously be disregarded, and to put it together in one book.

In the present age it is by no means easy for a journalist who is sent to Caldey to do a story, because, by virtue of their vocation, the monks can be elusive. When they are eventually located they are not often able to stay talking for long. At such times it must be very tempting to fill in the gaps by imagination. To point this out is only to refer to the present problem. Over the years references beyond number have been made to the church, the village church, the chapel, the Priory church and various other chapels and churches. Eventually we are faced with the question as to when is a church a chapel, or when is a chapel not a chapel, because some writers have been hopelessly misled and have had no idea as to which building they were referring.

Their confusion is understandable, and I would suggest that it is also forgivable. In 1925 there was published the *Royal Commission's Inventory of Ancient Monuments on Pembrokeshire.* Not only were there serious mistakes, but omissions. If such a body as this can fall short of the mark there is some excuse for us lesser mortals.

In *Total Community* I wrote for the most part of the fifty years on Caldey of the Cistercian Community there, and shall therefore try to repeat as little as possible of what I wrote in those pages. When the book was published there were those who expressed disappointment that I had not told more of the story of those who had lived on the island and struggled to make a living there over the years.

Life, of course, is about people. Without them no island or anywhere else can have a story. An island can be somewhere out there in the ocean for thousands of years, and frequented by countless thousands of sea-birds, but until somebody comes along to write about them, or talk about them, or film them, there is no story. Only then can the islands come to life. There have been far more people on Caldey than on the other Pembrokeshire islands, so there have been far more stories there.

Any one of another ten or a dozen people could write another ten or a dozen books about Caldey. I can only write my own book. Since *The Sounds Between* was published, very little has come to light about Skomer, Skokholm or Ramsey to lead me to think that it needs much revision, but as soon as this book is published, people will start telling me enough of what I have missed out to fill a couple more books.

The stories, of course, are different because, on the other three main Pembrokeshire islands, apart from the days of the early Celtic wanderers and settlers, there was only ever but the one farm and family unit with their servants on each island, whereas on Caldey there have, throughout the ages, been communities of anything up to a hundred people. So there have been far more stories of human endeavour, hardship and sorrow, success and failure, life and death, friendship and factions. Whatever may come to light as the years go by, much will have been forgotten and remain a mystery for all time.

For the last two centuries there is only one instance on record of anyone farming on the other Pembrokeshire islands for more than about ten years. On Caldey, there are many instances of people being born on the island, working all their lives there and eventually dying there. And this went on for generation after generation.

Perhaps something which will emerge in the telling of this particular story is the influence which the presence of a monastic establishment throughout the centuries has had, not only on the rest of the island community, but on the life of the surrounding area on the mainland.

Much has been written about Caldey over the years, and much is well-known. I am writing now for those who know the island and those who do not know it so well. There are, of course, thousands of such people, so the labour should not be in vain. Some know well enough by now, from any number of secondary sources, that the island lies south of Tenby, three miles from the harbour, and measures a mile-and-a-half in length and two-thirds of a mile in width. What they may not know is about its acreage, because this has been given at various times as something over six hundred acres and something under five hundred acres.

In the Caldey archives there is a document concerning the requisitions on title when Done Bushell purchased the island. The solicitors were puzzled by the fact that a conveyance and mortgage of 1894 had shown the size of the island as 609a-0r-32p, but the particulars three years later established the size of the island as 529a-3r-39p. Not surprisingly, their worst suspicions were aroused and they wanted to know what had happened to the odd eighty acres. Presumably they slept more easily when they received a reply to say, 'The difference is between high and low water marks, but the entire island is included in the sale.' It just so happens that, unusual though it may be, as the result of a grant dating back to Henry I, the foreshores on Caldey belong to the island and not to the Crown.

Another point which has not received as much consideration as it warrants is the fact that, when some of the old-time writers were describing the island and its approaches, Priory beach, as we now know it, hardly existed because, until the first half of the nineteenth century, the sea used to run right up to the beach adjoining the row of cottages in the village. Over the years since then the bay has silted up and the sandbanks have formed. Occasional shifting of sand from the beaches in Carmarthen Bay has always been a familiar happening. One set of weather conditions would carry huge quantities of sand from one beach to another and then, in due course, a contrary set of conditions would carry the sand back again. There is nothing as yet to hand in any estate records to offer enlightenment on the subject, but it would be interesting to know whether the marram grass, which grows in such profusion in the area of Priory Bay, could have been planted by human agency in order to reclaim the land, in the same way as it was done in the Laugharne estuary during the last century. The Benedictine monks planted some early in the present century, but there is no knowledge of its having been done earlier.

In the following pages I hope to fill in some of the gaps. In order to do so I have consulted many records and registers. By chance I came upon the fact that a gentleman by the name of David Oriel had died in 1924, at the age of eighty-four, in a house called Caldey Villa at, of all unlikely places, Aberbeeg in Monmouthshire. At least, it was in Monmouthshire before all the nonsense about Gwent and Dyfed and all the rest of it.

The *Census Returns* show that, in 1881, David Oriel was the farm bailiff on Caldey. Five years previously his son, William, had been christened in the village church, and that was just a few months after my mother's sister had been christened there, for my mother's father and mother made their first home on Caldey, where my grandfather was a gardener, and their first child, Margaret Eleanor, was born there. She died when she was nine, and my mother, who was born a year or two later, was named Eleanor after her. David Oriel was born on Caldey, where his father, Benjamin, was originally the carpenter and eventually became bailiff.

The reference to him was of interest to me because, for more than twenty years when I lived at Amroth, across the bay from Caldey, a descendant of that family was our next door neighbour, and her son, William, who also became a carpenter, was a star performer in the village boys' football team which I ran.

None of this, of course, is an essential ingredient for a best-seller, but I have learned the hard way as a writer that it is impossible to please all of the people all of the time, so if I please myself then I can be sure to please somebody. And, as I have already pointed out, this is my own book.

Chapter 2

Something of the sea-birds

More than one guide book has been written about Caldey by those who have sought to take the reader with them on a conducted tour of the island, and it is a commendable ploy. The only problem is that we all tend to see something different. 'Beauty,' as Thomas Hardy wrote, 'lies not in the thing but in what the thing symbolises.'

Someone who could watch for hours and be spellbound at the beauty of a fulmar petrel glide and swing across the cliff-face, may remain strangely unmoved to hear the monks chant at the lovely service of Compline at the end of the day. The man who could listen for hours to stories of what life on the island was like a century ago, would perhaps dismiss as a heap of old bones what remains as evidence of the existence of our far distant ancestors thousands of years ago. Worse still, perhaps, the man who would delight in this collection of remains of primitive man can be strangely unmoved by the deeds and difficulties and life-style of our more immediate ancestors, who are deserving of all our sympathy for the hardships they were called on to survive.

Not as much has been written about the sea-birds of Caldey as on this aspect of the other islands, although the birds will have been the same and the story much the same. In my book, *The Sounds Between*, I dealt at some length with the subject and also, in the second edition, with some of the plants and flowers of Caldey. A guide was published about sixty years ago, entitled *The Coasts of Caldey*, by James Wintle F.Z.S., and based on an article by him in the Benedictine magazine *Pax*, which was first published in 1904. It was useful insofar as it deals with the marine life and the botany, but it is best to draw a veil over the results of his many other references.

On all the Pembrokeshire islands, the guillemots, razorbills and puffins have declined terribly over the last century. There are still small numbers of guillemots and razorbills on the ledges of the south and western cliffs of Caldey, but only rarely is a puffin seen there nowadays. These birds, of course, apart from the depredations caused by oil pollution, have also been driven out by rats, as on Ramsey. There is no mention in any of the old guide books of the presence of rats on Caldey, but with the extent of the shipping trade there over the centuries, they could have been on the island a long time. There were some puffins breeding at West Beacon Point round about 1922 and a few more in the 1930's but, perhaps because of the presence of rats, it is probably years since there were as many sea-birds on Caldey as on the other islands.

One claim Caldey can make, however, is that, in 1867, a pair of swans were nesting on the old Priory fishponds.

An interesting point about the sea-birds was raised in *Mason's Guide to Tenby*, a well-known and most useful piece of work, published in the 1880s, when reference was made to the legend told of Caldey in the Breton *Life of Gildas*. According to some writers, St. Illtyd's Monastery and School were at Caldey. The Breton *Lives* of St. Samson of Dol and St. Paul of Leon, deal in similar vein with the same legend where, in the *Life of Gildas*, it said, 'The little Island was cribbed, narrow, bare and barren.' The school was so near the shore that at high tide the sea came in. Gildas, one of the students, was impressed with the power of prayer as he had heard it described by his master, St. Illtyd, on the text from Mark's gospel, (Ch. 11: v.24), 'What things soever ye desire, when ye pray, believe that ye receive them, and ye shall have them.' Gildas suggested to St. Illtyd that they should pray to the Lord Jesus Christ to enlarge the island.

This they did, and when they emerged from the oratory they found that the island had widened all round, and the barren soil had become fruitful. The next thing they did was to sow corn, but when it began to grow it was almost destroyed by the sea-birds. In turn the three lads, Gildas, Paul and Samson, were put to guard the corn, but to no avail. Eventually, again in answer to their prayers, they were able to catch the sea-birds and began to shepherd them towards the Monastery. When the Abbot came out of the oratory and saw them he marvelled at their faith and at the miracle which had been wrought. He charged them to treat the birds mercifully and, setting the birds free, bade them never again to lay waste to the Island's corn crops.

Mason then went on to say it was a curious fact that there was a certain wall on the island beyond which point the sea-birds had never been known to fly.

It is a nice story, of course, and it would be nice to be able to believe it, but it is also a fact that it would be extremely rare to find the auks fly far inland on any of the other islands. It is also in keeping with their habits in those places where they breed, or used to breed, on the cliffs of the mainland.

Mrs Fanny Price Gwynne, whose guide book appeared in 1852, also made reference to the sea-birds. Her references must be amongst the more reliable for her work was of high repute. She lived in Tenby where her husband was Town Clerk and Clerk to the Justices.

'This island,' she wrote, 'is the chief point of attraction to seaward, and in the summer months during the Tenby season, it is every day visited by parties who pic-nic on its beach or cliffs. The cliffs to the back of the island are at this time of the year frequented by numerous sea-fowl, of the species mentioned under the head of the "Stack Rocks". The eggs of those birds (razorbills and guillemots) are of brilliant colours and great variety, and may be procured of the cottagers on the island, who descend the cliffs for the purpose of obtaining them; they are of large size and make excellent puddings. The young birds of some of the species are also of excellent flavour, and when dressed as wild duck would scarcely be distinguished from them. Of an evening, the numerous flocks of birds may be seen hastening to their homes on the precipitous cliffs, whose rocky heights are literally covered by them.'

Before the uninformed start offering their opinions on the connection between the taking of the eggs and the decline of the sea-bird population, let it be pointed out that the gulls' eggs are still taken, as they always have been, in large numbers, and these scavengers continued to increase until recent years.

Occasionally, the gulls have been put to even better use than as providers of eggs, as when Br James, one of the monks, used them

Br James with the geese whose eggs he incubated with the gulls—Feb. 1953

Br James with the goslings after they had been hatched—June 29th 1953

as incubators for his goose eggs. He removed the gulls' eggs from their nests and introduced three goose eggs into each nest in their place. At twenty-eight to thirty days he was then able to look for the emerging goslings.

This is not something peculiar to Caldey, as it has been done from time to time by other islanders where the gulls have been nesting in such numbers for the nests to have spread inland from the cliff-tops to the more accessible flat ground. Murray Mathew, writing in 1894, made some reference to the practice in his book, *The Birds of Pembrokeshire and its islands.* In that instance he was writing of Skomer and referred to an occasion when the farmer on that island, Capt. Vaughan Palmer Davies, told him he had taken the eggs of a carrion crow and replaced them with hens' eggs. The crow hatched them out and, Capt. Davies said, the chickens were all black. What the casual reader, all these years later, would not know is that the old retired sea captain was an inveterate leg-puller. Maybe he even saw the enthusiastic old country cleric as the forerunner of that pestiferous brand of professional country-man destined to proliferate in the years to come. If he also fostered some fond notion of discouraging the proliferation universally of environmentalists, conservationists, ecologists and all the other species of that current growth industry, he fostered it, like the incubating crows and gulls, in vain.

The gulls would not have been the only predators of the eggs and the young of the sea-birds on Caldey. Caldey, like the other Pembrokeshire islands, has always been free of such predators as foxes, stoats and weasels. Like Ramsey, Caldey has for some time had its rats, but it also seems to have had its population of wild-cats. Although these prehistoric natives of Britain, which are not the ancestors of the domestic tabby cat which they resemble, were thought to have become extinct, apart from in the Scottish Highlands, by the nineteenth century, they were still on Caldey round about 1840. In that year, the owner of the island, Cabot Kynaston, was digging out a wildcat which had taken refuge at the High Cliff quarry, when he came upon what is now known as the Caldey 'Reliquary'.

In Murray Mathew's time, the cliff birds consisted of guillemots, razorbills, puffins and herring gulls. Manx shearwaters, he said, had formerly nested upon the island, and Mr Charles Jeffreys, of Tenby, believed that a few still did so in the fissures of the cliffs. Thomas Dix, a quarter of a century earlier, had spoken of large numbers of shearwaters on Caldey. It almost gives rise to speculation as to whether the rats arrived on the island as early as may be supposed, for the shearwaters and puffins would soon have been driven out by them.

Mathew then goes on to say that in the report of the *Migration of Birds*, as observed at Lighthouses, for 1881, Mr Ebben wrote from Caldey lighthouse: 'Though chough breeds upon the island, and never goes away.' If nothing else, it establishes the identity of one of the lighthouse keepers, for the *Census Returns* of that year do not give their names.

With its limestone to the northeast, and Old Red Sandstone to the southwest, Caldey has altered little since the days of the earlier writers, apart from the planting of trees by the Benedictines in the earlier part of the century and by the Cistercians more recently. There has also been the more pronounced change, due to the reclamation, if that is the word, of what was once the island's natural harbour behind the present-day sand dunes above Priory beach. Not much more than fifty years ago, according to Major Robert James de Carteret O'Neill, which was the name under which he wrote his book, *A Modern Pilgrimage*, and not his real name, under which he subsequently went to gaol, there was at that time a very old man still living in Tenby who could remember, as a small boy, landing in a boat at steps at the foot of the lime-kiln.

The one other point which, for the sake of posterity, must be referred to, is the assertion by the *Royal Commission on Ancient Monuments* in 1925 that Caldey was not 'completely separated from the mainland and transformed into an island until the period AD1500-1530, when a stupendous change had taken place in the land surface of Great Britain'.

Whilst I lay no claim to being competent to express an opinion on such a statement, I may be permitted to quote that very fine scholar, the late Arthur L. Leach, to whom the area owes so much. Reviewing the Inventory in the old *Tenby and County News*, he wrote, 'An Inventory issued by a Royal Commission necessarily becomes a permanent and authoritative work of reference for facts and for (presumably) well-based opinions. In years to come many of its statements will be accepted and incorporated in their books by writers upon the history and pre-history of the county—writers who will be unable to verify or estimate the value of the records. From its very nature this publication may never be issued in a revised and corrected edition. We therefore regret to find among assertions that are certainly ''more dogmatic than the facts actually warrant'' several that are quite surprising and misleading.'

Having demolished the assertion that the separation of Caldey from the mainland could possibly have been anything like as recent as the Commission suggested, Leach then went on to say, 'As geologists, professional and non-professional, are available who have closely studied the district, it seems unfortunate that the Commissioners did not consult with one before making this extraordinary announcement. He might have enlightened them upon the probability of this stupendous change which occurring according to them in the reign of Henry VIII, has left no record either in contemporary documents or on the coasts of western Britain.'

Leach then quoted Giraldus Cambrensis, who, living at Manorbier centuries before the date of the Jameston Survey of 1618 (quoted by the Commissioners), wrote of the 'island of Chaldey, which the Welsh call Inys Pyrr.'

'Again,' Leach continued, 'more than two hundred years before the supposed date of the separation of the island, in 1383 to be precise, certain men of Tenby seized on in Caldey Roads a great ship of Genoa laden with gold plate, sailed her into Tenby harbour, and there plundered her. But obviously Caldey Roads could not have existed before Caldey became an island. Finally, the very silence of George Owen, the historian, who visited Tenby and Caldey in the latter half of the sixteenth century, ought to have imposed caution on the Commissioners. For Owen must have talked with men who were alive during the period of this supposed "cataclysm". Yet the patient collector of facts, who describes the island, notes the depth of water in its anchorage and devotes a whole chapter of his great work to "Diverse Wonders of Pembrokeshire", has not a word to say of such a change which, had it occurred, would have been in his day a very living wonder. The Commissioners have incautiously misread the words which record (in the 'Survey') not actual observations but mere local traditions of the low marshy ground which, not in mediaeval times, but in prehistoric ages, linked Caldey with the mainland.'

And at this point we may reasonably proceed to our own examination of the story of Caldey, to the caves of which island the Atlantic grey seals still come to breed, as they have been doing for as long as the great Atlantic rollers have thundered against its towering cliffs.

Chapter 3

Early years

Nothing I could write would add anything to the knowledge of what is so far known of Caldey's earliest history. Some fine scholars and archaeologists have already covered the subject fairly comprehensively. And, life having existed there since something like at least 10,000 B.C., it is unlikely that anything new will come to light except in the further work of archaeologists. At that date Caldey was still attached to the mainland.

Later on, during the first few centuries A.D., it is evident that people occasionally lived in Nanna's cave, and in the hollow near the landing slip. Whatever evidence may once have remained of these early dwellers who came to the island to take the sea-bird harvest would have been removed by field clearances, as happened elsewhere, notably on the centre of Skomer. The field walls on Caldey, which go right to the cliff edge, would have been built of the stones of the primitive dwellings and enclosures of any earlier occupation. The extensive stone quarrying activities on Caldey also destroyed many valuable traces of that life which had once, long ago, been lived upon the island.

In the last century, for example, when quarrymen were working at Eel Point, they came upon bones of the Pleistocene period. They were shipped to Bideford where they were sold for grinding into powder for use as fertiliser. Other such bones included those of the hyena, reindeer, lion, wolf, Irish elk, bison, wild ox, mammoth, rhinoceros and hippopotamus from the days before Caldey became an island. Some of these bones were collected more than a century ago by a former rector of Gumfreston, the Rev. G. H. Smith, and subsequently became part of the collection on which Tenby's splendid little museum was founded in 1878. Their existence makes more interesting the fact that, of these early species, the wildcat survived until comparatively recently.

Something like three centuries after the last dwellers in Nanna's cave, about the year 500, which was half a century or more before

Skulls unearthed in 1916 and 1970

St. Columba's foundation of the isle of Iona, Celtic monks came to Caldey to live their austere life of prayer. From the name of Llan Illtyd, Monastery of Illtyd, given to the island in two of the old Breton *Lives*, it is apparent that these monks were a colony from St. Illtyd's Abbey at Llantwit Major in Glamorgan.

This fact has been so thoroughly established over the years that it may well not have warranted mentioning yet again had it not been for the fact that I recently discovered in the Caldey archives a letter from Mrs Dorothy Lyon, the youngest child of the Rev Done Bushell. It was undated, but probably written in 1951 to the Prior, and she said that, as she was now of advanced years, she felt she ought to place on record the fact that she had been told by the late Professor F. C. Burkitt, not long before he died, that he was satisfied that Caldey was not the island referred to in earlier writings.

Commenting on this, Dr F. G. Cowley, of University College, Swansea, says:

Was there an early monastery dating from the sixth century on Caldey Island? The Ogham stone with the Christian inscription on it certainly suggests that there was. Moreover, in the earliest extant *Life* of a British saint, that of St Samson of Dol (probably written between 600-25), the writer refers to an *insula* not far from Illtud's monastery at Llanilltud Fawr. The *insula* was ruled over by the aged abbot Piro. In course of time Samson, at the instigation of Bishop Dubricius, was given first the office of steward and then, on Piro's death, the office of abbot at this institution. Sir John Lloyd in his *History of Wales* (i, p.144, note 100) cautiously suggested that the *insula* 'may well have been Caldy Island (the 'Enis Pir' of Gir. Camb., VI, 92.)' The Rev W. Done Bushell was convinced that it was the island monastery mentioned in Samson's *Life* and incorporated this material into his article 'An Island of the Saints' published in *Archaeologia Cambrensis*, 1908, pp.237-66. Many reputable scholars have subsequently accepted the identification, including Dr Wendy Davies in her recently published *Wales in the Early Middle Ages* (1982, pp.143, 145, 151-2).

The letter in the Caldey archives from Mrs Lyon refers to a conversation she had with Professor Burkitt of Trinity College, Cambridge, before his death. Professor Burkitt was an old friend of Rev W. Done Bushell and had helped him in his researches into the island's history. He, too, was convinced in the early days of their association that Caldey was the Piro's monastery mentioned in Samson's *Life*. Later, however, he had second thoughts about the identification and in his conversation with Mrs Lyon said that 'I have entirely proved to my own satisfaction that Caldey could *not* have been the island mentioned in which Pyro became abbot and was followed by Samson.'

Professor Burkitt was an authority on the period and had contributed an important article on St Samson of Dol in the *Journal of Theological Studies*, vol. XXVII, 1926. But neither in the article nor in his conversation with Mrs Lyon did he give any reasons for his abandonment of his former views. One can, however, argue against the identification. Firstly, the word *insula* need not necessarily mean an island surrounded by water for it was frequently used as a synonym for monastery. Secondly, could a place, which in the sixth century would be four days journey from Llanilltud Fawr, be described as 'not far away'? Thirdly, the role played by Bishop

Dubricius raises problems. We are assured by scholars that some form of diocesan government existed in Wales at this period and Dubricius's activities in supervising monasteries has been adduced to support this view. But what was Dubricius doing so far from the main sphere of his activity which lay in south east Wales? Would he not have been infringing the jurisdiction of another bishop in making appointments to an alleged monastery at Caldey?

We shall probably never be able to say for certain that Caldey is the *insula* mentioned in the early seventh century *Life* of St Samson. It is, however, highly probable that some form of monastic life existed on the island of Caldey in the sixth and subsequent centuries. The islands on the Welsh seaboard offered a particularly attractive refuge for the monks and hermits of the Age of the Saints, and Caldey was as well placed as Priestholm, Bardsey, St Tudwell, Ramsey and Barry to provide such a refuge.

It is from before these times that the famous Ogham stone on Caldey dates. If there is one aspect on which I thought I would not have to touch, it is the Ogham stone, because so many scholars have expressed their opinions. As there have been so many doubts and differences between them, I am content to quote the work of Professor R. A. S. Macalister, who must be reckoned the final authority.

After dealing in detail with the stone's inscriptions, Professor Macalister goes on to say:

The latter part, from *rogo* onward, is fairly easy, the only difficulty being the sense to be ascribed to *ibi*. Is it a mistake for *hic*, 'here'. Or does it mean what it says, 'there'? Remembering that the stone is on an island, within sight of the mainland, we can understand how to the dwellers on the island, 'there' would become a natural expression for 'the mainland'. Such sentences as, 'There seems to be a fire over there', 'There is a boat coming from there,' etc. etc., would be in constant use. And one who wished for prayers might well express the hope that all those who came on pilgrimage to the island, and who returning, 'walked over there' (as he expressed it in his bad Latin), would not forget him: and, moreover, that they should carry out the duty *fervently*, which presumably is what he meant by *ex-orent*.

As to *singno crucis in illam fingsi*, we must understand *illam* as referring to the stone, and may explain its feminity by remembering that in Welsh, the language in which the writer was doubtless

thinking, *llech* is feminine. *Singno*, in which the attraction of the
legitimate *n* has nasalized the preceding *g*, may be interpreted in one
of three ways: 'By the sign of the cross which I have fashioned, I
pray'—a formula of adjuration; as an ablative: 'With the sign of the
cross I have' decorated it; or as a mistake for an accusative: 'I have
fashioned the sign of the cross upon it'. The last is preferable as the
simplest of the three possibilities: and the standard of Latinity which
it assumes is not too low for our author.

What, then, is the sense, of *et*? It implies that something has gone
before: but it certainly does not link on to the Ogham, with which it
has nothing whatever to do. Rather does it appear to link on to the
destruction of the Ogham. We may picture the writer as a hermit on
the island, occupying an anchorite cell which preceded the twelfth-
century priory. He discovered, and so far as he could, destroyed the
heathenish monument, left behind by some Goidel to pollute the
sacred island. Before doing so, he 'disharmed' the paganism of the
Ogham by surrounding it with crosses on all sides, as his fellow-
anchorites did on Inchnagoill and Inisvickillane; and he then found it
impossible to demolish the Ogham completely, without injuring his
own handiwork. In fact, the cross, which he had to cut on the dexter
edge before it occurred to him to hammer away the inscription
altogether, may have had much to do with saving so many letters on
that side from destruction. If the space on the stone had permitted,
and if his Latinity had been equal to the strain, what he would have
said would have been something like this: 'See, I have purged this
stone of its heathenism, and have fashioned the sign of the cross
upon it. I pray all who return to the mainland to make fervent prayer
for the soul of me, Catuoconus.' By this interpretation, the inscription is not the memorial of a dead Catuoconus, but of a Catuoconus no
doubt well meaning, but from the standpoint of an epigraphist rather
too much alive.

Apart from observing in passing that it is said that the worst
thing you can say about a man is that he means well, I would only
offer the additional observation that Emily Pritchard, in her
work, *The History of St Dogmael's Abbey*, thought that Catuoconus
could have been the Latin for Cathen, 'who lived in the latter half
of the seventh century; he was name-giver to Llangathen, and to
the hundred of Catheiniog, and may have been one of the early
Priors or Heads of the Religious House on Caldey.' John Edward

Lloyd put the added Latin inscription at about 750 A.D. and as referring to Cadwgan.

About the best of the books to have dealt with the early history of Caldey in its first religious period must be *Isle of Caldey*, published by the Cistercians in 1931, drawing as it does on the earliest known works.

According to the Breton *Life* of St Samson, St Dubric, Dyfrig, or Dubricius, one of the greatest of the Welsh saints, used to come to Caldey to keep his Lenten fasts. He came from the Valley of the Wye, where he established a school for clerics and a monastery. Afterwards he was to become the first Bishop of Llandaff, before eventually retiring to the island of Bardsey, where he led a life of solitary prayer with his disciples until he died at a very great age.

Whilst these early Celtic monks were on Caldey, monasticism was spreading and flourishing on the Continent. It was in Italy, early in the sixth century, that St Benedict wrote his famous Rule for monastic life, which is still observed by the Cistercians on Caldey today.

That first monastic settlement on Caldey would have grown as each newcomer arrived to build his own cell, in the tradition of the day, probably of wattle, round the chapel. Certainly the site chosen would have been the site later to be chosen by the mediaeval monks, because that was the site of the abundant spring of water which is still the main source of supply for the island.

The first Abbot of the Caldey monks was Pyro, and it was from him that the island almost certainly took its Celtic name of Ynys Pyr, or Isle of Pyro. Doubts have been expressed on this suggestion from time to time, and I have myself been guilty of doing so, but, having had the opportunity to go into the question more thoroughly, I cannot seriously entertain any longer the other possibilities. Other islands were also named in those early days after different saints. Ramsey, for example, was known as Ynys Tyfanog, and sometimes, by the Welsh as Ynys Dewi. Bardsey, during the same period, was associated with St Cadfan.

Pyro was followed as Abbot, after his untimely death, by St

Samson. With Caldey being a daughter house of Llantwit Major, both of these abbots would have been appointed by St Illtyd.

Much was written about Caldey in the various *Lives* of St Samson, and it is from them that the story came of Pyro's death, it being recorded that, 'One dark night this same Piro in an unseemly drunken bout, as they say—which makes matters worse—wandered alone into the precincts of the monastery and fell into a deep well. He raised a shout of distress, but when he was rescued from the water by the monks he was almost dead, and so he died that night.'

The story and the sin, note well the 'they say', would have lost nothing in the telling as time went by. It never does. Who was it said that man changes but little, God never? By the Middle Ages a certain Guibert de Nogent (died c1124) is said to have reported the following, 'I call God to witness, that I have read again in utter loathing to them that were with me—in the Life of Samson, a saint of great reputation in France and Brittany, concerning a certain abbot whom that book names St Pyro. When, however, I sought into the latter end of this man who I held for a saint, I found his special mark of sanctity to be this; to wit that he fell into a ''well'' while drunken with wine, and thus died.'

Can we not imagine what sort of impact would be made by such a story if the same thing happened today? For my own part, I prefer the attitude of the local chapel deacon, returning home one Saturday night, when he had taken a few too many on board and fell asleep in the ditch. A little while later his own minister came along, shone his light on him, shook him awake and, in tones of good, old-fashioned nonconformist outraged piety, said, 'John Phillips, chapel deacon! What would you say if you found me in such a condition as this?'

To which his deacon replied, 'Not a mewk to a soul! Not a mewk!' Mewk is Pembrokeshire for a small sound.

For the record, the scholars reckon that Pyro was more likely to have fallen into the pond than a well.

Although St Samson did not remain long on Caldey, he has always been the island's patron saint. The various *Lives* of St Samson have considerable authority because they were based on an original memoir of Enoch, whose uncle was a near kinsman of Samson's, and who had himself conversed with the saint's mother, Anna.

St Samson, a native of Pembroke, was offered to God by his parents, Amon and Anna, at an early age, and sent to St Illtyd's great school at Llantwit Major.

St Illtyd (450-535), born in Brittany, was ordained priest by St Dubric, and with the assistance of a Glamorgan chieftain, Meirchion, founded his great school of learning, known as Llan Illtyd. Here came the sons of many a British chief, and among the scholars were St Paul Aurelian, the first bishop of Leon, St Gildas the historian, who founded a monastery on the Ruys peninsula in Brittany, and probably the great St David as a boy, although as a youth he was at Tŷ Gwyn. These Celtic lads were taught, not only the truths of their Faith and the ways of virtue, but farming, irrigation, building, and the arts of medicine and surgery learned by St Illtyd from the Druids.

According to one account St Illtyd, in his youth, served as a knight of King Arthur's court. The glass in the window of the south side of the nave of the mediaeval Priory church was designed and made by Dom Theodore Bailey, one of the Benedictine monks on Caldey in the 1920s. It shows St Illtyd as a young knight being warned in a dream by an angel to return to the holier life of his boyhood.

After St Samson had been ordained priest by St Dubric, he came to Caldey to seek a life of greater austerity, solitude and prayer. It was possibly some years later that he became Abbot, and then, shortly afterwards, he went to labour in Ireland. Seeking a still deeper solitude, and a means to escape the fame of his miracles, he returned to a cave somewhere on the banks of the Severn.

Reluctantly, he left this retreat of prayer to be consecrated bishop by St Dubric, leaving Wales and setting sail for Brittany. His signature is to be found among those attesting the Canons of the third Council of Paris in 557, and his journeyings took him to the Channel Islands, of which he is one of the patron saints, but it was in Brittany that he worked his great apostolate.

Caldey was probably the stopping place for traffic between

Brittany, South Wales and Ireland, for the early Celtic saints were also sailors. There is evidence, too, that part of the old mediaeval priory had in fact been built in the period of Celtic settlement, corroborated by a similar evidence of Celtic ruins in Ireland. It is also believed that part of the north wall of the sanctuary of St David's, the village church, dates from the 6th century.

At Dol, St Samson founded a monastery and became its first Bishop. It was there, too, probably in 565, that he gave up his blessed soul to God. The contemporary Breton *Life* says that monks far off praying in their cells beheld the glory of his soul, and that, when they had laid him to rest on the Gospel side of the high altar, angelic music filled the air, drowning the voices of the choir, while the tomb was surrounded with a heavenly light and gave forth a fragrance which filled the church.

In 1919 a small part of St Samson's relics was sent to Caldey, where the Abbey and its church are dedicated to him.

At this juncture it is perhaps pertinent to remember that Christianity was brought here by the Romans. At various times Roman coins have been found on St Margaret's, the little island between Caldey and the mainland, known at one time as Little Caldey, but this is not to suggest that they could have been anything but passed from hand to hand by British folk.

The religion brought by the Romans is far more significant than any coins which have been found on the odd occasion. In nonconformist Wales it is not readily appreciated perhaps that these early Christians of Caldey were in fact Catholics. There are those, of course, who would dispute this, so again we can only turn to the scholars on the subject, in this case J. E. De Hirsch-Davies, who wrote in his *Catholicism in Wales*:

> Before we proceed to the evidence of later writers of mediaeval Welsh literature in general, it will be worth our while to dwell for a moment on the picture of early Celtic Christianity, drawn by Gildas in the 6th century. Gildas, the author of the *De Excidio Brittaniae*, written in some Glamorgan monastery, did not profess to write history. He was a religious and ecclesiastical reformer, and he inveighs against rulers and clergy in a savage and merciless spirit. But in spite of the violence of his language, his writings are very import-

ant, for they contain valuable information bearing on the religious condition of the times.

Professor Hugh Williams has dealt very fully and critically with the evidence of Gildas in his *Opera Gildae*, and in his *Christianity in Early Britain*. We cannot do better than quote his estimate of the various historical *questiones vexatae* that emerge from this pregnant period in the history of the Celtic Church. Most of the leaders of the nation, spiritual and political, come under Gildas's unsparing lash—and among them Maelgwyn Gwynedd, the *draco insularis*, who was in charge of the defences of the country.

Taliesin was chief bard to Maelgwyn at his court in the fortress of Deganwy, in North Wales. Gildas was himself a monk, and monasticism was already established in the country. In fact, it would seem that it was the religious world outside the monasteries that Gildas criticised so unsparingly.

Now, what has he to say of the Church in his age in Celtic Britain? What was its Faith? Its ministry? Its relation to Rome?

In the words of Willis Bund, was the old Welsh religious system a kind of foregleam of modern Nonconformity?

The historical evidence must decide what the answer is to be, and the evidence is conclusive. Professor Hugh Williams, who was a thorough Protestant, writes as follows (*Christianity in Early Britain*), 'About A.D.400 we find that there was in all Christian lands the idea of one Church, called the Catholic Church. Membership of this Church, whether for individuals or for communities, was dependent upon the acceptance of the Faith, and upon general conformity with the existing ecclesiastical order'.

The writer admits that the conception of St Peter, contained in the words, 'caraw voli Pedyr', is found even in Gildas. Passages in the *De Excidio* show that no other conclusion is possible.

In his *Epistle*, e.g., Gildas writes in his usual vein of the priests in Britain: 'Britain has priests, but they are foolish, unsurping the *Chair of Peter* the Apostle with (their) unclean feet.'

. . . In the *Vita Gildae* he himself gave an account of his pilgrimage to Rome 'to invoke the merits of the Blessed Apostles Peter and Paul, that by their intercession he might obtain from the Lord pardon for his sins'.

These, then, were the early Christians who established the tradition of prayer on Caldey, and could have been there until the coming of the marauding Norsemen.

Whilst there is not only no evidence that Caldey was pillaged, it is also as well to remember that a monastic establishment is not self-perpetuating. After the peak period of the Celtic monks there was a falling away, and monasticism on Caldey could have been on the wane by the time of any such raid, if it occurred at all.

Chapter 4

The mediaeval monks

The first recorded raids of the Vikings along the Welsh coast were not until the 9th century. In 795 the monasteries at Lindisfarne and Iona were plundered by Norsemen, and it is possible that Caldey could have been sacked shortly afterwards, but there is no evidence of this.

It is well to remember, however, that the hated Saxons were also on the rampage at the same time, and the Welsh were only too pleased to welcome the Norsemen, to absorb them into their culture, and even to Christianise them. It should not be assumed, therefore, that, even if the monks on Caldey had been killed, the island remained as a base for sea robbers.

Whether any Christian presence or influence survived on Caldey after any possible slaughter, there is no knowing, but certainly from 800 onwards the piratical character of the Norse raids along the Welsh coast changed to one of conquest and colonisation and to peaceful maritime trade. It is also pertinent to point out that, in spite of the various archaeological activity on Caldey, no evidence of the Norsemen's presence has ever come to light.

Bearing these facts in mind we can look with more understanding at the Norse name, Cold Island, from which Caldey has been derived.

As far as I have been able to ascertain, it was W. D. Bushell, junior, the son of Done Bushell, who first put forward the idea that the name came from the Norse 'Keld', meaning a spring of fresh water. Like his father, he became a schoolmaster and was a man of scholarship. But, like his father and the rest of the family, he also had a great affection for the island, and could hardly come to terms with the thought that anyone could think of their beloved island, with its benign and mainly frost-free climate, as being cold. So it is understandable that he should have sought some other explanation.

27

The indisputable authority on this subject, however, is Dr B. G. Charles, and I would be no more likely to try to teach God theology than to question his interpretation. Elsewhere I have given his reasons for maintaining that Caldey in its original form meant Cold Island.

Further than this, however, more than half a century ago, in contradicting Bushell's suggestion, Professor A. Mawer, director of the survey of English Place-names, remained convinced that the meaning of the name was Cold Island, but agreed with a suggestion that it would be in the sense of uninhabited, vacant or unattractive.

Between 795 and 1157 Pembrokeshire witnessed twenty-one raids by sea-rovers. Given that some of the raids took place at the same time, and were carried out by the same operators, there would have been lengthy periods when they were nowhere in evidence. It was the peaceful traders themselves over these years who gave their alien names to Caldey and other islands round the coast.

Initially, however, the activities of the raiders caused a prayer to be included in the Litany, 'From the fury of the Norsemen, O Lord, deliver us.' Whilst there must often have been apprehension, it would be misleading to assume from this a continued presence.

How long after any initial pillage it would have taken for people to reoccupy the island can only be a subject for conjecture. Unlike the other Pembrokeshire islands, however, where there was ever only the one household, there is evidence, which will be discussed later, that on Caldey there has for long been a number of households and, consequently, a community. Likewise there is evidence that the eggs and young of the sea-birds were taken for food. In those days of poverty and bare subsistence, therefore, it is unlikely that the island would have been abandoned for long. It is equally certain that the bare subsistence farming as practised on the mainland would also have been carried on there.

It is when we come to the 12th century that we find documented evidence as to what was happening on Caldey, and the need for mere conjecture is considerably reduced. Certainly the island could not have been without some value and significance, for in 1113 it was the subject of a grant by Henry I to one Robert Fitzmartin, the son of Martin de Turribus, or Martin of Tiron.

This first Martin, Lord of Cemais, is a shadowy figure but nevertheless a real one. He was not designated Martin de Turribus (or Tiron) until the antiquaries of Tudor times applied that term to him, believing that he had come to Britain in the wake of the Conqueror from Tiron in France, and he may well have had connections with that place. He seems to have been known as *Martinus de Walis* ('of Wales'), and as such was first witness to the foundation charter of Totnes Priory, and was possibly so called because of his connection with Cemais which he and his son Robert subdued. All that is known about him otherwise is that he married Geva, the daughter and heiress of Serlo de Burci, a tenant in chief at the time of the Domesday Survey in Somerset and Dorset. Martin was dead by 1086, for his widow had already married William de Falaise by then. Done Bushell was almost certainly in error in deducing from the writings of William of Worcester that Geva was Martin's mistress and not his legally wedded wife.

In his last years Martin turned to religion, and laid plans for the building of an abbey at St Dogmael's, but died before his vision could become a reality.

His eldest son, Robert, who had succeeded him as Lord of Cemais, granted Caldey to his mother, Geva. When Martin died, Robert and his wife, Matilda, were of one mind that Martin's plans should be continued with and the abbey was completed in 1118 on the site of the religious house founded by St Dogmael, who is reckoned to have died about 500 A.D., and which at one time had been under the rule of St Dubricius (Dyfrig).

The new abbey having been completed, Robert arranged with William, the Abbot of Tiron, to send over an Abbot and thirteen monks for its foundation. St Dogmael's thus became the first dependent Abbey of Tiron, and Robert endowed it richly with certain lands in St Dogmael's and other lands in Devonshire, and Matilda gave them Moylgrove. The Abbey was dedicated to St Mary in honour of the Holy Mother of God and ever virgin Mary.

The mediaeval priory

Within a few years a monastery, dedicated to St. Mary, and closely following the customary plan, was established on Caldey, which in 1131 was formally granted to the abbey by Geva. She had a sister who took the veil at Shaftesbury during her father's lifetime.

From certain documents of the early 14th and late 15th century it is clear that from the time of the original grant the Crown retained certain rights.

The new Priory on Caldey was built on the site of the earlier, more primitive, establishment and was a place of some substance which still remains. To judge by its loop-holed stairways and battlemented towers it was clearly built with defence in mind. Nearby was the spring of fresh water and, near this, a big pond was made. Quite possibly this pond had already been made by the earlier monks, but the newcomers no doubt improved it and also made two more ponds lower down. The ponds were stocked with fish. A little further down, a corn mill, powered by the little stream, was built, and the remains of this, including the millstones, are still clearly in evidence. The new lay-out also included walled-in gardens.

Remains of the mediaeval corn mill and millstones

Done Bushell reminds us that the island was for some time in the possession of Robert Fitzmartin, and postulates the theory that it was probably he, therefore, who built the oldest part of the Priory for his own protection, and that this was later incorporated in the monastic buildings. It is a thought well worth considering and seems to be a logical explanation of what was happening at that time.

At the same time as this work was in progress a round watch tower was built on the cliff-top above Priory Bay. From here, no doubt, warning of approaching danger could be signalled to the Priory. For a long time now this tower has been converted to other use and is at present the chapel of Our Lady of Peace. Fflorens Roch, in her little book, *The Isle of Caldey*, wrote that there were also the remains of another watch tower, subsequently incorporated for use as a lime-kiln, on the other side of Priory Bay, nearer to the quarries.

Still plainly visible in the Priory church is the cobbled floor of pebbles inlaid on end. It was a custom, generally believed in

The watch tower and quarry before St. Philomena's had been built
(Photo: Tenby Museum)

The Priory church with its cobbled floor

Pembrokeshire to have been brought by the Normans, which lived on in the county throughout the ages, but this is a surviving example of what must have been one of the earliest occasions for it to have been used.

There is no record as to how many monks were at Caldey at that time, but the Priory had been built for about a dozen or thirteen monks. Giraldus Cambrensis, who was born at Manorbier, and must have known the monastery well, was critical of the fact that monks at Caldey, as well as elsewhere, were living as solitaries in defiance of papal decrees.

What could also be of interest was the way in which the monks and any other people on the island earned their living for, as we shall see, there certainly were other people living on the island, and it was a period when monasteries were to become wealthy.

Herring catches at that time were heavy, and the Caldey oyster beds were renowned. It has been notable throughout history that the farming of the Pembrokeshire islands has always followed the same pattern, so that much the same thing would be happening on the islands at any one time. Although records are few and far between, where they do exist for one island, it is a reasonably safe assumption that the same sort of thing would also have been happening on the other islands.

For Ramsey, towards the end of the 13th century, there are figures to show that the farming being carried on was extensive. No such figures are available for Caldey, but there is a reference in the Taxatio of Pope Nicholas for 1291—'The Church of Caldey (belonging to the Abbey of St Dogmael's) £3-6s.-8d. Also he hath at Caldey one carucate of land with rent of assize £1-10s.-0d.' The intention was to raise money for the Crusades.

A 'carucate' was as much land as could be turned over by one plough in a season. Possibly it would have been about fifty acres. There would have been goats for cheese-making and, as always on the islands, a fair head of sheep.

In the Patent Rolls, Oct. 20th, 1306, there is a record of 'Letters for the Abbot of Tiron, staying beyond seas, nominating Gorwaretus de Caldey and Thomas Godhyn his attorneys for five years. By fine of 100s made in chancery.'

It is perhaps permissible to speculate whether Gorwaretus was Prior, and it is certainly of interest to see such a good old Welsh name as Gurwared there.

Henry Owen, in his Calendar of Public Records relating to Pembrokeshire, has found only brief mention of Caldey. In the accounts illustrating the Memorial History of the Earldom of Pembroke and its members (1326-1546), we have, for 1326-31, 'Account of John Le Herde and John Methelan, reeves of Pembroke from Michaelmas 1326 to Michaelmas 1327. Rents -4d, toll of one ship coming to Caldei this year, and no more; tolls of the port of Milforde, nothing this year because it seized into the hands of the king along with the town of Haverfordwest, and the tolls are extended at 8s.'

Also, in 1327, there is in the Patent Rolls, (Westminster, Jan. 30th), 'Protection, with clause *nolumus*, for one year for the prior of Caldeye.' There were more than twenty other characters so listed, including one who was going on a pilgrimage to Santiago.

In a way, this protection was a kind of early-day mafia, but as it was in the name of the king it was rather more respectable. Usually such protection was applied for by someone going on a long journey. Local troubles in South Wales could have made such a request for protection via royal officials necessary. The clause 'nolumus', meaning 'we do not wish' signified that the 'letters of protection' had a clause attached.

'Letters of protection', and licences to trade, were frequently granted to the mediaeval Cistercians in Wales with just such a condition attached—'So long as they do not aid the king's enemies.'

The 1327 protection in the case of Caldey, however, was of a common type, and was one of a large batch issued at the beginning of the new reign, the first instruments of all to be enrolled on the patent rolls of Edward III. The letters of protection granted to the Prior of Caldey merely safeguarded additionally the goods and property of the monastery. The original clause had read, 'We do not wish, for instance, that any of the corn, hay, horses, carts, wagons, food or other goods or chattels of the said prior, be taken, against his will, to our use, or that of others, by our bailiffs or ministers or anyone else who-soever.'

What could be of more interest is why the letters of protection were necessary at the time they were granted.

For the Ministers' Account, 1390-1, we have, 'Small tolls, 2s.-1d.; toll of houses and of castle, 16s.-11d.—namely Carrew, 7s.; Maynerbir, 4s.; Stackpoll, 12s.; Castlemartyn, 5s.; Calday, 3d., this year.

'Kiltoll of ships calling at Pembroke, Calday, Crystewell, Angulum, and Marchaltwye, NIL. Custom of fish at Calday, nil. And know that the Earl of Pembroke ought to have from each ship calling within the port of Milford, Marchaltwye, Cristewell, Angulum and Calday, 4d; and from each load, 2d., *wherever* they called on the lord's land within the county of Pembroke.'

Lastly, for 1480-1, the same apparent lack of enthusiasm for paying taxes and tolls is evident for the same ports. No customs fell 'of wine, salt, herrings, wool or boats at Pembroke, Caldey, Carissewall, Marchelowy, and Angle, or of fish taken at Caldey, because no such customs were taken; ditto for the customs of iron and millstones.'

As yet, there has been no reference in the records to something of very great significance to the farming and finances of the island, and that is the introduction of rabbits. They were brought here by the Normans and introduced to the other Pembrokeshire islands about 1300. It is quite certain that they would have been introduced to Caldey at the same time. For seven centuries since then rabbits have figured prominently in the finances of all the islands. Originally they were a great delicacy, protected and costly. Not least was the hidden cost of the immense amount of damage they did to the pastures.

In mediaeval times they were bred in conygers (rabbits were known as conies) or rabbit banks and, just across the water from Caldey, what is now Tenby's Esplanade was built on such a conyger cliff. Rabbits were a source of revenue, and nowhere more so than on the islands. I have written so much elsewhere about the tremendous impact made by the introduction of rabbits to the islands that I do not propose to repeat the arguments here, but the importance of the subject cannot be over emphasised.

Apart from these references for the period, the information on Caldey is slight. Fortunately, perhaps, Leland in the early 16th century, is mercifully silent on the subject, for he was notoriously confused in his references to all the islands. Even in the case of Caldey he managed to site Pill there, when it was actually at Milford.

Some of his notes were based on hearsay, and this was inevitable and understandable in an age when travel and communications were slow and difficult. The same probably applied to William of Worcester more than half-a-century previously. Writing of Caldey in 1478 he said that there were thirty houses there. Writers beyond number have quoted this figure *ad nauseam* and I am sorry to have to admit that I have been guilty myself. Yet it requires little serious thought to realise that it has to be nonsense. There is no indication that William of Worcester visited Caldey, and it must be extremely doubtful that he ever did. Had he done so he would have had more to say of it.

If anyone entertains doubts on the subject let them ask the first hundred people they meet in Tenby how many houses there are on Caldey in this present year of grace and just see what sort of answers they will get. If it had been said that there were in fact thirty people living on Caldey in 1478 that could have been much nearer the truth. It is known with far more certainty that only fifty years or so later there were no more than about nine houses there. Who would have had the enthusiasm, and for what purpose, to pull down twenty houses in the intervening years?

I hope that if any writers of the future come out with the statement that in the 15th century there were thirty houses on Caldey, they will also quote their source and that it will be somebody other than dear old William or those who have been misled by him.

Chapter 5

Last years of the mediaeval monks

No record has ever come to light of the number of mediaeval monks on Caldey at any one time during their existence there for more than four hundred years, but the probability is that, certainly in the later years, they were very few, and may only have been there in the capacity of stewardship for the mother house of St Dogmael's.

During the Wars of the Roses there was a long gap when nothing could be gleaned about St Dogmael's or her cells, until 1504. On July 16th of that year, during the reign of Henry VII, there was a visitation at St Dogmael's. The Abbot, Lewis Baron, was questioned and diligently examined concerning the state of his Abbey. He testified that it was in good order, free from debt, and that his four bretheren were of good conversation, honest and obedient. Dom Nicholas, Prior of Caldey, who was also examined, corroborated this evidence.

In the Episcopal Registers of St David's Vol II, there is mention of a Royal writ appointing collectors of a church levy in 1511 of four tenths of the income to be collected in four instalments from 1512-16. The church of Caldey was amongst those excluded.

In 1517 there was another levy of two tenths of the income. Again Caldey was amongst those churches excepted and . . . 'Also the temporal goods of the abbot and convent of St Dogmell in the deanery of Kemes in the same archdeaconery are excepted by authority of convocation on account of the excessive poverty and ruinous state of the said monastery.'

If that was the state of the mother house, the foundation of Caldey was unlikely to have been any more prosperous. And, in addition to the Priory, was there also a church on Caldey?

The island had remained in the ownership of St Dogmael's from the time of Henry I until the dissolution of the monasteries. In the Valor Ecclesiasticus of Henry VIII (1535-6), the cell of Caldey

38

contributed £2-3s.-4d. annually to the mother house, its annual value being £5-10s.-11d. plus tithes of 11s.-11½d.

It is with the suppression of the monasteries that we find the first detailed account of what was happening on Caldey, even to the identity of those who were living there.

The first account in the Ministers' Accounts for King Henry VIII, 1535-6, shows that at the surrender of the house there were nine tenants on Caldey holding by lease or by the year. From their names they appear to have been a fair mixture of Welsh and English.

Tenements in the island of Caldey demised to Thomas ap William Owen by deed as it is stated	7s.-4d.
Tenement with appurtenances demised at will to John Williams	7s.-4d.
Tenement with appurtenances demised at will to John Whyting	6s.-0d.
Tenement with appurtenances demised at will to Richard Prowte	5s.-0d.
Tenement with appurtenances demised at will to Lewis Whyting	8s.4d.
Tenement with appurtenances demised at will to Thomas Prowte	5s.-4d.
Tenement with appurtenances demised at will to Lewis Webe	4s.-0d.
Tenement with appurtenances demised at will to William Gough	10s.-0d.
Tenement with appurtenances demised at will to John Adam	3s.-6d.
All titles with the site of the priory of Caldey, containing by Estimation 18 acres, demised at will to Owen Lloyd	60s.-0d.
Total	£5-16s.-10d.

As was noted in the previous chapter the fixed rents in 1291 produced 30s. per year, so it comes as no surprise to find that in 1535 the monastery still had tenants farming the land. At that time there were many regional differences in the case of land tenure and usage, but George Owen, writing round about 1600, had much to say which suggests that hereabouts the stock were grazed communaly.

> For I have by good account [he wrote] numbered three thousand young people to be brought up continually in herding of cattle within this shire, who are put to this idle education when they are first come to be ten or twelve years of age and turned to the open fields to follow their cattle, when they are forced to endure the heat of the sun in his greatest extremity to parch and burn their faces, hands, legs, feet and breasts in such sort as they seem more like tawny Moors than people of this land. And then with the cold, frost, snow, hail, rain and wind they are so tormented, having the skin of their legs, hands, face and feet all chaps (like chinks of an elephant wherewith he is wont to take the flies that come thither to suck his blood), that, poor fools, they may well hold opinion with the papists that there is a purgatory.

Each of the Caldey tenants would have had his own little enclosure and, for the rest, the island would have been well suited to the communal grazing described by Owen.

It is of interest that in his book, *The Welsh Church—From Conquest to Reformation*, Professor Glanmor Williams points out that at the dissolution there was only one monk on Caldey. Given the knowledge that there were nine tenants farming the island between them, it is easy to accept that the one monk would have been there as a steward on behalf of the mother house.

There is one other important point to remember. Up to this time, and for a long time afterwards, rabbits were the property of the landlord. Throughout this period there are many records for the other islands which show the tremendous importance and financial value of the rabbit crop to the owners. If the accounts for St Dogmael's Abbey were ever to come to light it is as certain as anything can be that Caldey would prove to have been no exception. The tenants would have bemoaned the damage being done by the rabbits to the pasture for which they were paying rent, but the landlords would have had their eye only on the easier and quicker shilling.

Who the solitary monk was is not known. Caldey was in the archdeaconry of Cardigan and therefore its Prior attended St

Dogmael's for all visitations and signed his name after the Abbot of St Dogmael's. Therefore, in the signature to the Act of Acknowledgement of the King's supremacy, Dom Hugh Eynon may have been the last Prior of Caldey. This, however, was only supposition on the part of Emily Pritchard for she also points out that, from the date of its being granted to St Dogmael's Abbey by Geva, little is known of its history. Its seal is no longer to be found, neither is there at Westminster any Act of Supremacy signed by the Prior and monks of Caldey. In the light of all the other considerations her suggestion as to Dom Hugh Eynon has considerable foundation.

There is the further pertinent thought that the extra-parochial status of Caldey, which continues to the present day, could date from the times with which we are now dealing. In the mediaeval period, when the island belonged to St Dogmael's, the mother house and its island domain were not subject to the ordinary jurisdiction of the Bishop of the diocese of St David's over his parochial clergy, although he possessed the right of visitation, whenever he considered the circumstances called for the exercise of his authority. Certainly from about this time the island seems to have been set adrift from parish affairs and legislation.

In notes on Caldey in the Pembrokeshire Records Office, Francis Jones points out that Caldey is not mentioned in any of the Lay Subsidies of the 16th and 17th centuries, and no one seems to have been worried about its exact status.

Details of the ownership of the island are fairly well documented. Originally, following the dissolution, it was leased by John Bradshaw, of Presteigne, who acquired St Dogmael's and other property in north Pembrokeshire. Amongst various reprises was a stipend of 72s.-6d. payable annually for 21 years to the 'chaplain celebrating divine service and having cure of souls in the chapel of Caldey.'

Particulars of the grant also make it clear that the island was previously tenanted by a number of people, with reference also to farms in the plural. Now, however, it was all to be in the tenure of the said John Bradshaw. The tenants, of course, would have remained. The only difference for them was probably the fact that they now had a new landlord.

It is, of course, important to remember that, although it is possible to trace the ownership of Caldey from the original grant to Bradshaw right through to the present day, for much of the time the land there was let to a tenant or tenants. The various owners did not necessarily live on the island. To build up a picture of the people living on the island is quite a different matter.

For example, in the Subsidy Rolls for 1542-44, there was reference to 'Portions of the account of the first payment of the subsidy granted in the 34 and 35 Henry 8th, upon the inhabitants of the Hundreds of Narberth and Castlemartin.' The Hundred of Castlemartin included, 'Caldy parish: Thomas Perrote, in goods £4 . . .' and the tax collected was 8d.

Perrote was probably, therefore, Bradshaw's tenant, And, spelling of names being what it was at that time, it is perhaps not idle to speculate as to whether he was the Thomas Prowte listed as one of the tenants in 1535.

Following the dissolution there is no further reference to be found anywhere for St Dogmael's until 1544, in Dugdale's 'Monasticon', with reference to a memorandum of the desire of John Bradshaw to purchase the Abbey of St Dogmael's, together with the parcels and possessions belonging to it in South Wales.

The King, in return for the sum of £512-2s.-10½d., handed over St Dogmael's and Caldey, and received back the 21 year lease of 1538-9, granting a fresh lease for 21 years. Thereafter Bradshaw simply paid a tenth of the yearly value to the king.

John Bradshaw died in 1567 and Caldey passed to his son, John Bradshaw junior. Presumably the lease was renewed for, in 1579, the existing lease was cancelled, a new lease granted for the balance of the 21 years of the old lease, and an additional 21 years, with remainder to his son, William Bradshaw, his heirs and assigns for their lives.

Throughout this time Tenby was prosperous and was to remain so up to the time of the Civil Wars. Something of this prosperity would have influenced what was happening on Caldey. In 1579 we also find the first reference to rabbits. In the Plea Rolls for that year there is reference to 'John Browne of Tenby against John Bradshawe Esq. for the seizure of 200 rabbits worth 40s. at Caldy and other iniquities.' Whatever else it may or may not indicate it does at least show the high value of rabbits at that time, for they were probably catching a couple of thousand or more annually. Probably Browne was the tenant and had caught the landlord's rabbits, amongst other of his shortcomings as a tenant.

Then, in 1604, again in the Plea Rolls, there is the case of John Webb of Caldey Island, yeoman, defendant against Rice Thomas and his wife Jane who, before her marriage in 1603 was possessed of goods in the hands of the said John Webb, and was married at Penally to the said Rice Thomas, and the said John Webb detained the said goods. We cannot know what this dispute was all about, but it establishes that John Webb was a yeoman and, therefore, a man of some substance.

Once more it may be permissible to speculate as to whether he was a descendant of the Lewis Webb of 1535.

Chapter 6

After the Suppression

Later on, it could be of interest to examine in more detail some of the many references to churches or chapels on Caldey, but before doing so it is worth remembering something of the religious background to what was happening and to be aware of the intolerance.

As we saw in the last chapter, George Owen put the papists pretty low in his reckoning. And John Bradshaw, on taking his lease on Caldey, had to pay £3-13s.-6d. a year for a chaplain to cure souls in the chapel of Caldey, from which it would appear that the crown reserved the right of presentation to the chapel, no doubt in the first fine flush of enthusiasm and determination to bring these papists into line.

Whether it means anything I have no idea, but, in his *Church Book of Tenby*, Edward Laws says, 'There is a document preserved in the Record Office called "Surveys of Wales, Elizabeth and James 1st" in which, under the head of "Chauntries in Tenby, AO.R.Re.Eliz.xxvl," is the following passage: "Will Caldey, by an indenture made to him (by) one Robert Collins, formerly vicar of the parish church of the Blessed Mary, in Tenby, and also feoffe of the lands, keeper of the Chapel of Jesus under the church, dated 10th July, in the year of King Henry VIII, 30" 1538".'

In the same book, Laws refers to the fact that in 1636 John Owen received his licence under seal from Roger Mainwaring, the Bishop of St David's, to say prayer and perform all duties pertaining to the office of curate and deacon in the Church of Tenby and Caldee.

A century later William Howell, in 1758, seems to have performed the same duties. He was called *curatus perajendus*. But that is to be going too far ahead.

Right from the start the Welsh refused to accept the new religion being forced on them by England, and for a century and a half continued to resist. Maybe it was why the Welsh were so ready in

44

due course to become dissenters or nonconformists. Many hundreds died for their faith. Six of them are honoured in the Calendar of Saints. It is no purpose of this work to discuss that aspect in great detail, but it may not do us any harm to read again what the judge said when sentencing St David Lewis, the last of them—'David Lewis, thou shalt be led from this place to the place from whence thou camest, and shalt be put upon a hurdle and drawn with thy heels forward to the place of execution, where thou shalt be hanged by the neck and cut down alive, thy body to be ripped open and thy bowels plucked out; thou shalt be dismembered and thy members burned before thy face, thy head to be divided from thy body, thy quarters to be separated, and to be disposed of at His Majesty's will. So the Lord have mercy on thy soul!'

It is good to know that the monks now go up to the old Priory church for Vespers sometimes on the Saints day for the Forty Martyrs of England and Wales. We may be quite sure that if God does, as He surely does, have mercy on their souls, it would not be at the behest of the monster who pronounced such a sentence.

How far any of this attitude may have impinged on life on Caldey there is no knowing, just as there can be no knowing how well the various curates carried out their responsibilities for the curing of souls.

There was a school of thought as recently as Emily Pritchard's time that Caldey was such an out of the way Priory that possibly it was never dissolved separately from St Dogmael's. It was averred by a Roman Catholic still living (1907) that the monastery continued to exist early in 1700, and that it was the last place in Great Britain where Mass was celebrated, excepting in private chapels.

The other aspect of life at the time, which would have had some effect on the islanders, was the presence of pirates in the coastal waters. The anchorage off Caldey had long been acknowledged as good. An early reference is, 'A pamphlett conteiginge the description of Mylford haven with all the good rodes and harborowes thereof . . . described this present yere of our Lord God 1595 By George Purefoy of the Countie of Warwick.' Of Caldey he said, 'The harborowe is verie good save only when the winde bloweth strongly at southeast a high east wind is naught but not so bad as the southeast, for it is worste, but upon all other windes there is safe riding there.' It was probably this survey George Owen was quoting in a similar reference.

After the reign of Queen Elizabeth, for forty years from the accession of James I in 1603 to well on in the reign of Charles I, the Severn Sea became infested with pirates. In 1565 the Privy Council appointed the Bishop of St David's and Dr John Vaughan of Carmarthen members of a commission to suppress piracy in Carmarthen Bay. The Bishop was Dr Richard Davies, the translator of the New Testament, a man of tremendous energy. Reference has already been made to the building of the round watch tower, and it has often been mentioned that what is now known as St David's church has signs of having been used by the islanders to barricade themselves against the attacks of pirates.

Perhaps one of the most frequently quoted writers on this subject has been that remarkable man, George Owen, and his writing is always cited to illustrate the terrible depredations of the pirates on Caldey. So there is perhaps no harm in quoting him just once more, only this time examining more carefully what he really had to say.

'The island is very fertile and yieldeth plenty of corn. All their ploughs go with horses, for oxen they dare not keep, fearing the purveyors of the pirates, as they themselves told me, who often make their provisions there by their own commission, and most commonly to the good contentment of the inhabitants when conscionable thieves arrive there. The island is of eight or ten households, and some part of the demesnes annexed to the ruins of the priory the lord keepeth in his hands. It is now grown a question in what hundred of Pembrokeshire this island should be, whether in Cemais as parcel of St Dogmael's, to which it appertained, or part of the next hundred of the main, and until this doubt be decided the inhabitants are content to rest exempt from any payments or taxations with any hundred . . . There is adjoining to this Great Caldey a small island placed between it and the land called Little Caldey. It beareth good grass for sheep and conies, and store of gulls.'

The bit most writers love to quote, and I have been guilty of it myself, is about the islanders ploughing by horses because they were afraid to keep oxen in case the pirates made off with them. Well, at least, that means they were ploughing, and Owen had already stated that the island was very fertile and yielded plenty of corn, so they were not without hope. Lime-kilns were much in use for burning lime for the improvement of the land and as fertiliser.

But did he not say much more? Did he not say that the purveyors of the pirates made their provisions there by their own commission?

It was a time when all sorts of people, including the squires and magistrates, are known to have acted in collusion with the pirates and smugglers and freebooters. The pirates had agents everywhere. What better place than Caldey for them to call to take on supplies of food? Far easier for them to trade for it than to have to catch and kill their own. By trading for it they could be sure that there would always be supplies there for them. As far as the islanders were concerned, how much more convenient to sell direct to the pirates, without having to hump their sheep or cheeses or any other produce across to the mainland in order to dispose of it. No wonder Owen was able to write that the whole business was 'most commonly to the good contentment of the inhabitants.'

In 1633 there is record of a typical raid by pirates on Ramsey, and there is no doubt that such raids took place from time to time. But it was not all on the debit side, and no doubt Caldey, with its larger population, was much less vulnerable than the other islands, each with its solitary farmhouse. The pirates would have been ready to bully and steal, but they would not have welcomed a stand-up fight each time they wanted supplies.

No doubt their purveyors would have threatened and done some arm-twisting, wherefore the islanders would have deemed it prudent not to keep oxen to attract too large a landing party. But they probably considered it a fair price to pay not to invite too much trouble.

Nor should it be thought that life was one long struggle by those of the land against the depredations of those who came by sea. As mentioned in reference to Leach earlier, on May 30, 1383, there was a, 'Commission to Simon de Burley and James Lyons, serjeant at Arms, upon information that certain of the king's subjects of Tenby by the isle of Caldey within the county of Pembroke in Wales have seized a great ship of Genoa laden with two barrels of gold plate and other merchandise, taken it to Tynby and are removing the said cargo, to enquire touching the circumstances, and if the same are the goods of friends, to restore them, or their value, in accordance with the tenor of a mandate under the privy seal herewith sent.'

An interesting observation, in passing, is Owen's reference to Little Caldey, as St Margaret's was then called. Apart from the sheep, there is also mention of the conies (rabbits), which only confirms what has already been discussed. And it seems, too, that the sea-birds and their eggs were also being exploited.

Earlier, in his reference to Caldey, Owen said, 'It did belong to the abbey of St Dogmael's and was purchased by Mr Roger Bradshaw, father of the last Mr John Bradshaw, grandfather to Mr John Bradshaw that now is, who about four years past sold the same to Mr Walter Philpin of Tenby, whose inheritance now it is.'

I do not know where he thought Roger Bradshaw came into it. Oddly enough, Fenton refers to George Bradshaw as having purchased Caldey after the dissolution. Elsewhere he refers to John Bradshaw's death in 1588 and says, 'To this John Bradshaw, at the dissolution of the religious houses, this abbey (St Dogmael's) was granted.' Again he was not quite right, for the John Bradshaw, junior, who died in 1588, was the son of the John who was granted St Dogmael's and Caldey, before purchasing them, as we have already seen. The John Bradshaw who sold Caldey to Walter Philpin was, as Owen said, the great-grandson of the man who first held the island after the dissolution. He was born in 1574 and died in 1634.

The really interesting reference, however, is to the fact that Walter Philpin, who was mayor of Tenby in 1601, had purchased the island about four years previous to Owen's writing.

In this will dated Dec. 12th, 1610, Walter Philpin made, amongst others, the following bequests: 'The island of Caldey which I

lately bought of John Bradshaw Esq I give to my wife Elizabeth . . .
The manor of Erewere lately mortgaged of Robert Elliott Esq, to
be enjoyed by my son, Henry Philpin.'

The reference to Erewere is of interest to me because that was
the old name for Amroth Castle where I lived for more than
twenty years in sight of Caldey across the bay.

Walter Philpin was another of the owners who would not have
lived on Caldey but, from Owen's reference to the fact that the
lord kept some part of the demesnes in his hands, it would seem
that, in those years of prosperity, he would have spent some part
of the year there, probably in the summer.

Chapter 7

Enterprising developments

Up to this time herring catches were still heavy and the fishing generally was good. A celebrated fishing ground, which had played an important part in the history of Tenby's fishing trade, was known as Will's Mark. In 1627, John Rogers, who was at that time mayor of the town, asked the old fishermen 'to nominate unto him as near as they could what were the marks that was holding to be good to find out the said Rock and these parties delivered as followeth . . .'

The fishermen's names were—John Brown, John Adams, Thomas Adams, John Moore and William Kethin and their instructions were 'to bring the high hill of Neath on Port Eynon head, and Caldey Chapel on the old Windmill of Tenby.' This reference will be of more interest in another context later.

Tenby's prosperity was based in those Tudor times on sea-trade and wool and merchandise. This prosperity must have had some effect on what was happening on Caldey. It all came to an end, however, with the Civil Wars. Cromwell laid siege to the town and, in 1643, it was attacked by land and sea for three days. It again fell to the Parliamentarians in 1648. As if this were not enough the Plague swept the town in the middle of the century and from then on it was of no economic consequence. Even in the first part of the 19th century it was still in a ruinous state.

Under the terms of Walter Philpin's will Caldey passed to his grandson of the same name.

In 1642 an indenture is recorded between Katherine Johnes, alias Philpin of Bonvilles Court, widow, on the one part and Thomas Bowen of Trefloyne, gent, and Thos Lloyd of Saint Issells, gent on the other part. The nature of the business is not clear, but it is more than likely that the island was being let, and presumably to Thomas Bowen. Katherine was probably either Walter Philpin's daughter, or the widow of his grandson Walter, and subsequently married a Johnes of Bonvilles Court.

In 1653 Katherine Johnes, otherwise Philpin, together with Devereux Johnes of Bonvilles Court and Bridget, his wife, sold Caldey to Reeve Williams of Llanridian in Gower and Robert Williams of Loughor. A merchant, Richard Brown of Pembroke, was a party to the covenant. The Williams family were to hold the island for another one hundred and thirty three years.

It seems that Reeve Williams, at any rate, lived on Caldey, for, within ten years, the naturalist, John Ray, visited the island and wrote, in 1662, 'We passed over to Caldey Isle, of which Mr Williams is owner, and were civilly received there. In the Island are three chapels, one at the Abbey or Priory, and two more.'

During that same decade we have a reference in Francis Green's catalogue of Wills for Nov. 3rd, 1668, 'Administration of the goods of Reece (sic) Williams of the Island of Caldey, was granted to John Gold of the parish of Loughor, Glam, his relation to the use of Richard and Jane the children of the deceased.'

Shortly afterwards, in 1684, in the Pembrokeshire Plea Rolls, there is reference to one Walter Jenkins of Tenby, otherwise called Walter Jenkins of Caldey, who was summoned to answer the suit of Thomas Walters in a plea of debt of £10 which he owed and unjustly detained. The actual debt was £5, but the bond to secure the payment was in the sum of £10.

It would seem that by this time the Williams family had given up farming the island and that possibly Jenkins was doing so, albeit not living there but employing others who did.

Shortly afterwards, in 1693, we find an 'Indenture between John Williams, of Tenby, gent, on the one part, and Daniel Poyer of Grove, in the parish of Narberth, farmer and Thomas Child of the parish of Begelly, gent.'

It is clear that the younger Williams was by then living in Tenby and it also suggests that he was letting the island, in this case to Daniel Poyer. The next reference tends to confirm this.

It is an interesting reference to be found in the *Treasury Papers* for 1708. At the Court of St James's on May 3rd that year a petition was received from 'Capt John Williams, Commander of a Sloop attending the Custom House at Bristoll, and setting forth, That a French Vessell, called the *St Peter*, was some Time since wreckt on the Island of Caldy (the Petitioner's Estate) and that he hath recovered of the said Wreck some Pieces of Cable and Timber and Two Small Gunns and their carriages, which he humbly prays a Grant of towards Defending and Repairing the Losses the aforesaid Island hath sustained from the French Privateers . . .'

In March the following year there is a record in the *State Papers* that his petition had been granted. Coastal dwellers are not traditionally so scrupulous about reporting upon wreck which they have salvaged, but as Capt. Williams was in charge of a sloop attending the Custom House, he no doubt thought that it behoved him to set a somewhat better example. He died at Bristol in 1730.

It was later in the same century that we first hear tell of visitations to Caldey by another privateer, the notorious Paul Jones. Born c.1749 in Kirkbean, on the coast of Kircudbright on the shores of the Solway Firth, the fifth and youngest child of a head gardener, he went to sea at the age of twelve. Of a rebellious and violent nature, he returned for a time to his father, before joining a band of smugglers and then, with money thus acquired, buying a small vessel. He manned his ship with desperate characters and began his life of piracy.

Eventually, when England had become too hot for him, he crossed the Atlantic and threw in his lot with the American insurgents. Of a poor moral character, he was nevertheless a fine seaman of great courage, and became an enthusiastic and sincere partisan in the cause of the colonists.

The legend has always been on Caldey that he used to come to the island for water and, to do so, anchored in what is still known as Paul Jones' Bay. The stories of his visits to the island were first told at times which were sufficiently recent to have much basis in fact. As will be seen later, there were people living on the island in the first decade of the present century whose forebears had lived there for generations beyond number. Whether any credence can be given to the story that when Paul Jones died c.1792 he was buried on Caldey, his body being pushed into a crevice in the rocks near Ord Point, is another matter.

By about 1748 the fishing industry had declined enormously, and the whole of the first half of the century was a black time for the farming community. The system of the day was wasteful, with a tendency for farmers to slaughter many animals in the autumn because of lack of greencrop and roots for winter feeding. Although they were liming the land, having small numbers of live-stock they were also short of manure. In any case, with most of the island open to grazing, there was not much land available for the conservation of hay.

From the middle of the century things began to improve. It is known that on the other Pembrokeshire islands the field enclos-ures took place at this time. Although we know nothing of what was happening on the land on Caldey, there cannot be any doubt that here, too, laying out of the field system as we now know it, was begun at this time.

Lewis Morris's map of 1748 shows Windmill Tower near Priory Bay. Subsequently this was converted to use as a lime-kiln, the remains of which still stand near St Philomena's, and this conversion may or may not have taken place at the same time as the field enclosures as part of the improved farming practice. We have to remember that there was also the other lime-kiln on the other side of Priory Bay.

At this point, as we shall presently see, the Williams family were not farming the island themselves, and it can also therefore be open to question whether they were living there.

Certainly, for 1764 and 1768, there are indentures to show that the island was let to John Stokes of the parish of St Thomas, Haverfordwest, gent.

In 1771 the tenant was Frances Skyrme, Esq. of Llawhaden, who held a considerable acreage of land in south Pembrokeshire at that time, and there is the more detailed reference to '. . . one manor, 6 messuages, 10 tofts, 600 acres of land, 40 acres of meadow, 100 acres of pasture, and 200 acres of furze and heath in the island of Caldey in Tenby, and the tithes thereof.'

Caldey had long been a manor in its own right. A messuage was a house with some land and perhaps outbuildings attached, whereas a toft was a cottage. But is there anything in the wording of this document, insofar as it relates to acreages, to suggest that it was somewhere about this time that work was starting to enclose land with stone walls, before further work began on laying out the field system with walls?

In the National Library of Wales there are three interesting hand-written diaries. The first, by one S.S. Banks, tells of an excursion to Wales in 1767. An entry for September of that year reads, 'Went off with the mornings tide for Calde, a small island about a League from the Shore, it contains about 500 acres by guefs, is let for 100 a year: the middle parts are fenced in with a strong wall, and yield Corn and Pasture: the outside is everywhere full stocked with Rabbets. There is in the middle of the Island the remains of a very good House, with a Chapel belonging to it, the whole of very ancient Construction, & almost down.'

Throughout these centuries, the farmers or gentry who rented the island to farm it would not have lived there but would have had shepherds and herdsmen working there.

The second diary is of an unknown traveller who, for August 20th, 1787, wrote, 'Sail to Caldy. Some of the rocks round the back of the island are curious. One house two bushes & a willow tree are to be seen there. The rent is £100 per ann which the tenant pays chiefly by means of the rabbits with which the whole place abounds.'

In the Pembrokeshire Records Office there is a lease which was deposited ten years ago with the County Council by Mr T. Loveday of Banbury. From this it is not only confirmed that Caldey had been sold in 1786 to the Earl of Warwick for £3,000, but that a lease of 1778 between the Rev. John Henry Williams of Wellesbourne in Warwickshire was part of the marriage settlement of John Williams and his wife, Sarah Warner. Caldey, in fact, was being used as an investment.

The Rev. John Henry Williams who sold Caldey to George Greville, Earl Brook and Earl of Warwick, was a great-grandson of Reeve Williams who had bought the island in 1653. The Deed of Exchange included the sale of: 'All that the Manor or Island of Caldey in the county of Pembroke with all messuages etc—Wrecks

Goods and chattels of Felons. Felons of themselves, Fugitives and Outlawed Persons, Waifs, Estrays . . .'

The Earl of Warwick purchased a great deal of property during his life, and was continually either selling or exchanging lands in one county to increase and consolidate his holdings in another. Unfortunately, he had trouble with his solicitors, and the whole of the documents for a period of about twenty-five years were lost.

His ownership of Caldey was brief for, in 1798, he sold it to Thomas Kynaston of Pembroke.

Whilst all this was happening, the farmer, from at least as far back as 1776, was one David Llewellyn. In the old church register of Penally there is an entry to show that he married Mary Rowe, a spinster of that parish, on June 1st that year, at which time he was given as a farmer of Caldey Island.

Of much greater interest than that, however, is an agreement dated March 12th, 1798 on the occasion of the purchase of the island by Thomas Kynaston. It said, 'Articles of Agreement between David Llewehellin of Caldey Island, co. Pembroke farmer and Thomas Kynaston of the town of Pembroke county Pembroke, esquire. In consideration of £900 to be paid to David Llewhellin Mortgages all that the island of Caldey. From date of these presents Thomas Kynaston shall and may . . . enter upon the said island and premises and erect raise and build any messuages Tenements Erections and buildings on any part of the said Island of Caldey (except the present dwelling house) and shall and may in like manner import and land coal and culm for burning lime-stones Timber Slate and all other articles necessary for building and digging Stones And also shall and may from time to time and at all times dig Limestone and open Quarries on all or any part of the said Island . . . also that the said Thomas Kynaston shall and will on or before the Tenth Day of April 1799 pay or cause to be paid to David Llewhelin a moiety or one half of the nett produce of the sale of all such rabbits as shall be taken by Thomas Kynaston in the said island between the 10th Oct. next and 2nd Feb. 1799. Such Rabbits to be taken in the same number and quantity as David Llewhelin has been accustomed to take . . .

Thomas Kynaston exclusively lodging and maintaining a man for taking the same.'

Some of the references in this agreement speak volumes without any comment being necessary.

To go ahead of the story, it is interesting to find that, in the National Library of Wales, there is reference to a case in Chancery in 1833 of Bowlas Summers against James Summers, John Mathias and John Evans. What they are doing in a case concerning Caldey would not normally be immediately clear. However, it so happens that, during those years, three of the same people were also involved in the financial affairs of the other Pembrokeshire islands of Skomer and Ramsey, where they had bought out the interests in various leases and mortgages. It looks very much as though they had a finger in the Caldey financial pie as well.

The 'ingoing' which Thomas Kynaston had agreed to pay David Llewellyn was £566-18s.-7¼d. By 'ingoing' we mean payment for stock, crops and implements of husbandry. There were also other items by way of interest on the mortgage, and £50 'cash produced by sale of rabbits.' The total came to £697-16s.-9¼d.

Against this there was a contra account from Thomas Kynaston, including cash already paid, leaving a balance due to David Llewellyn of £398-7s.-6¼d.

This account had been settled and 'acknowledged to be just and fair' and signed by Thomas Kynaston, with David Llewellyn making his mark, on Oct. 10th, 1799. A bond had been given for the £398 and the residue paid in cash.

By 1833, however, the money would appear not to have been paid and, in support, George Llewellyn, son of the late David Llewellyn, 'who had occupied Caldey for twenty years prior to 1798', testified to the financial arrangements according to the agreement, and further testified 'that the said Thomas Kynaston continued to occupy the Island from the year 1798 to the time of his death and that his sons had continued to occupy it ever since.'

From 1790 to 1815 generally, as a result of the Napoleonic wars and duty on imported corn, farming fortunes improved, and it was a time of investment. All the islands tell the same story.

Kynaston added a handsome mansion to the Priory about 1800, and possibly some farm buildings also date from this period.

With church records and *Census Returns* becoming available from early in the 19th century the story unfolds with more detail.

Chapter 8

The church of Our Lady, and St Margaret's

Before looking more closely at life on the island from the beginning of the 19th century onwards, it would perhaps be useful to consider some of the innumerable references to the church and chapel. And I say this, because there has been so much confusion caused by the various references to church, priory, chapel and village church, that it is sometimes difficult, if not impossible, to know to which building reference is being made.

When sorting out the notes for this chapter I was tempted to start by quoting what appeared to be the best reference. And I yielded to temptation. Unfortunately, the author is unknown, but the article appeared in the winter edition of *Pax* in 1923:

> In the Itinerarium of William of Worcestor, written at the end of the fifteenth century, occurs the following passage (ed. of 1778, p.155)—
> Insula Caldey sequitur proxima Shepey iland corcum villa Tynbye per unum miliare . . . et est circa 30 domos populatas, et unam turrim, cum capella Sanctae Mariae super maris litus, ac ecclesia prioratus de Caldey fundata (Martino) cum amasia sua.
>
> For the following reasons the chapel referred to was the village church.
> 1. It is unlikely he would mention a tiny chapel or shrine and say nothing of the much bigger building which was *de facto* (though not *de iure*, as the island was extra-parochial), the parish church;
> 2. he could reasonably refer to this 'village church' as *capella*, both in distinction from the *ecclesia prioratus* and because it was, in fact, a chapel and not a parish church—in the few documentary references that there are both the priory and Village churches are apparently called church and chapel indifferently;
> 3. at the time William of Worcester wrote, *capella . . . super maris litus* would describe the position of the village church as well and better than that of the building at Chapel point, for in those days the sea came to within a few yards and it was literally on the sea-shore, whereas the other stood 180 feet above the sea, where there is no *litus*, properly speaking, even at the lowest tide.

The same view was taken by A. L. Leach in an article in the *Tenby and County News* in 1942.

There would be no point in dwelling further upon the subject were it not for the fact that Done Bushell came along and wrote, in 1908, 'We are told on good authority that where the lighthouse stands there was a chapel of the Blessed Virgin. It is referred to by William, Bishop of Worcester . . .'

Well, of course, in all fairness to William of the thirty houses of revered memory, he said nothing of the sort. As we shall see later, it was Done Bushell, and a marvellous man he was, who brought the Benedictines to Caldey about that time. Guided by him they probably knew nothing of the village church's earlier dedication to Saint Mary on the Seashore, and thereupon dedicated it to St David. To avoid any further confusion it would be well to refer to it from here on by that modern name.

What, then, is there known of the chapel on the cliff? When the lighthouse was built in 1829, it was on the site of this little chapel, and probably the stones were used in the new building. Although so little is known of it, there cannot really be any doubt that it was a typical anchorite's cell. As Fenton wrote, 'Every insulated rock off the coast had its cell and its anchorite.' There was probably one on St Margaret's, certainly one on St Catherine's and another on Monkstone, which first appeared by that name on Saxton's Map of 1578. The remains of the foundations are still there.

These anchorites often had indulgences for acts of charity granted to them by way of favours to do penance for some sin or other. In the case of the little chapel on the cliff at Caldey it would have been the fairly obvious service of keeping a beacon for the benefit of seafarers. There was probably also a garden there as well. The map to a Schedule of 1897 shows such a garden beyond the confines of the lighthouse, the remains are still to be seen, and it is highly unlikely that anyone else would have elected to make a garden in such an exposed position. The point below the lighthouse is still known as Chapel Point.

It is likely that this was the 'Caldey Chapel' to which the old fishermen were referring in 1627 when giving their directions for locating Will's Mark, although it is just possible, but hardly likely, that they could have been referring to the spire of the Priory church at a time before the lighthouse had been built. The chapel was also clearly there when John Ray visited Caldey in 1662.

Wintle, for what it may be worth, said that, 'according to local tradition, it had survived down till 1748.' He does not give his source, but the point has already been made that there were people on Caldey at the time of his visit whose ancestors had been there for many generations. They may not have known much about *capella* and *maris litus*, but they knew what their fathers had told them, and their fathers and grandfathers before that. And, after a lifetime's association with such people, I would pay more heed to what they have to say than I would to all the professional countrymen who are always ready to sneer at them.

1748, of course, was also the date of Lewis Morris's map, and he showed the 'Chappel seen from Sea,' so that this may have been the original source of Wintle's second-hand information. The date does seem something of a coincidence.

There is one other thought. If there is anything in the story handed down to Emily Pritchard, that Mass had been said on Caldey until early in 1700, could it just be that it was not in the Priory chapel, as she thought, but secretly to the faithful out there on that lonely cliff top sanctuary?

To revert, then, to St David's, as we now call it, the church on the seashore. Done Bushel wrote in much detail on the building itself with its many Norman features.

The north wall of the Sanctuary dates from the 6th century, and it was probably here that the islanders, as distinct from the monks, had their first place of worship. Certainly it was here over the ages that they were laid to rest. Everywhere in its environs bones have been, and are still, found. There is reference in the *Transcripts of the Carmarthenshire Antiquarian Society* XII, 43, ill, to the finding of stone coffins when they were digging the grave to bury Dom Gildas, one of the 20th century Benedictine monks. The graves were formed by two or three slabs at the bottom, on which the body was laid, and then surrounded by slabs arranged as a rectangle, the whole being covered by more slabs. It was a

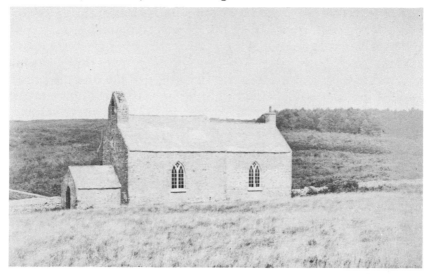

St. David's Church before its last restoration
(Photo: Tenby Museum)

common practice for the burying of ecclesiastics and prominent personages in the 12th and 13th centuries.

When what is now the village school was being built, a skeleton was found and moved into the 'ossuary' grave in the nearby churchyard. When graves are being dug in the churchyard these days it is not unusual to come across skeletons at two or three feet deep and, sometimes, again at five or six feet. About twenty years ago a couple of monks, including Fr Robert, the current Superior, were digging for loam, for Br James' bedding plants, at a spot outside the churchyard and to the north of the church, when they came across a whole heap of bones, so they packed up and went and dug somewhere else.

It would seem, therefore, that St David's was the focal point for the islanders' worship since time out of mind. Done Bushell was of the opinion, from his own observations, that it could possibly have been built in the twelfth century on the lines of an earlier Celtic church, incorporating some of the original walling. The opinion has also been expressed that the square holes on either

side of the entrance could have been made to take the ends of a
strong wooden beam when an attack was being resisted.

It is difficult to guess what use may or may not have been made
of the church during the 17th and 18th centuries, but Fenton,
who did at least visit the island, somewhere in the first decade of
the 19th century, said, 'To the right of the road going down to the
beach, there is an old chapel, in which till lately, there stood a
baptismal font.' Although he does not say so in as many words,
his references to the Priory church paint a picture of neglect and
decay. For a while what is now St David's church saw service as a
blacksmith's shop and that could well have happened round
about this time.

In 1838, however, Cabot Kynaston, who had succeeded his
father, Thomas, restored the building to a certain extent and it
was pressed into part-time use as a dame school. There are interesting references to this but, even now, unless and until further
information should come to light, we cannot know the whole
story.

Reporting on the state of Education in Wales in 1847, the Commissioners appointed for the purpose said, 'There is a building
used as a church when any clergyman chooses to go over and
serve it, but there is no regular service or minister. The proprietor
does not permit the use of this building to Dissenters. Two or
three years ago there was a clergyman visiting Tenby who used
without payment to perform service in the church regularly, but
since his departure the practice has not been maintained. The
proprietor considers that the endowment or establishment of a
church might compromise his privileges of being extra-parochial
and tithe-free. The present Bishop of St David's has offered him a
bond of indemnity in both respects, but the offer was not
accepted . . . There had been a private dame-school kept in the
island, but on the dame's death no one succeeded to her post.'

At the time of the Report there were 39 children on the island,
27 of them being between the ages of 5 and 15 years.

If we turn now to Mary Anne Bourne's *Guide to Tenby and
Neighbourhood*, published in 1843, she says that, in spite of the
island's ecclesiastical history, including a church and a chapel

(long since in ruins), no edifice of the kind had of late years existed on the spot. I incline strongly to the view that by the chapel in ruins she was referring to the Priory chapel. The chapel on the cliff had, by her time, disappeared, the lighthouse having been built upon the site in 1829, coinciding with the building of Saundersfoot harbour.

She went on to say, 'A benevolent clergyman, residing in the neighbourhood of Tenby, Rev Mr Greaves, has, however, taken strong and unwearied interest in the moral and religious welfare of the cottagers and their children. A small plain building was erected near the shore, a few years since: and every Sunday, when the weather was not too tempestuous to admit of crossing over from Tenby, he has continued to resort thither for the purpose of conducting divine service, and instructing the poor tenants of the island.'

Who, then was the Rev Mr Greaves? I have asked myself the question many times and am still no nearer to finding the answer. History could well prove me to be as wide of the mark as William of the thirty houses. I make no assertions, therefore, but offer what facts I have been able to find.

I have been able to find nothing of a Rev Greaves in the 1851 *Census Returns* for Tenby, but in the *Tenby Observer* weekly list of visitors on June 15th, 1855, there appeared a Rev Talbot Greaves and his wife of Cheltenham. That worthy gentleman assisted Dean Close at Cheltenham from 1854-6, having previously been vicar of Mayfield from 1850-4, when he seems to have moved down to Weymouth. He was born in 1826 and died in 1899.

In the Journal of the *Archaeologia Cambrensis*, 1870, Albert Way, referring to the Ogham stone, said, 'The slab has been removed and fixed in the wall of the chapel on the suggestion of an archaeologist, by whom its value would be truely appreciated, the Rev James Graves.'

Way, however, was quoting from the original article by Professor O. Westwood of the *Arch.Cam.* of Oct. 1855 and the original article did not say the Rev James Graves but the Rev Mr Graves. Scholar though Mr Way must have been, I beg leave to entertain certain reservations because, in his same article, in

1870, he said that Caldey contained thirty families. That magical thirty! Where have we heard that figure before, and how often shall we have to hear it again? The 1871 *Census Returns* show that there were sixteen families there. By 'the chapel' Way was referring to St David's church.

The only other reference comes from Fanny Price-Gwynne, in 1852, when she says, 'There is a small plain building near the shore, where occasionally a clergyman (a friend of the proprietor) performs the Church service, and a school for the cottagers' children is held here.'

The chances are that the Rev Talbot Greaves could have had some connection with the island but, if he is our man, he could not have had anything to do with the restoration of 1838 because, at that time, he was only twelve years of age.

At a slightly later period, services at St David's are said to have been taken by a Tenby draper, according to the useful little book, *Caldey Monastery Isle*, by the late Derrick Harries, a one-time colleague of mine. Apart from moving Prinknash from Gloucester to Devon in a moment of mental aberration, such as caused Leland to move Pill from Milford to Caldey, and being oddly confused about the location of the fish-pond, Derrick was not the sort to have made his statement about the Tenby draper without good grounds for doing so. I know he had talked much to older, local people, about the island's history. By the time of which he was writing, Cabot Kynaston, with his earlier reported dislike of Dissenters, had been called to higher realms, and Caldey was in other hands. And could it, perhaps, as we shall see later, have been a grocer rather than a draper, who was the occasional preacher?

Of the identity of the school dame, just prior to the Commissioners' Report in 1847, we can be more certain. The 1841 *Census Returns* show that she was Margaret Moody, who lodged with Thomas Webb and his family. The registrar's entry shows that she was found drowned on Caldey on May 26th, 1843, aged 37, and the Penally church register shows that she was buried on May 30th of that year, aged 40.

The 1851 *Census Returns* make no mention of any school mistress, although Mrs Gwynne, two years later, was quite definite that a school for the cottagers' children was being held. Unfortunately, the Caldey sheets for the 1861 *Census Returns* have been lost, so there is no way of checking for that year. A decade later, however, in 1871, the schoolmistress was eighteen years old Sarah Oriel, youngest of Benjamin Oriel's large family, and sister to the farm bailiff, David, who made his appearance in the first chapter. Reference can be made to the Oriels later.

Of the other church and chapel references it only remains to deal with the Priory itself. As with St David's, bones seem to have been all round it in profusion. For the four or five centuries of the first monastic establishment, and the four centuries or so of the mediaeval Benedictines, all the monks to have died would have been buried somewhere near their monastery. For a few years at the beginning of this century the Priory chapel was used for Anglican worship by the villagers, but there is nothing to suggest that at any other time would it have been used by anybody other than monks.

Unaware of the earlier dedication to St Mary, the Blessed Virgin, the Benedictines, after Done Bushell had restored it in the early part of this century, dedicated it to the Celtic St Illtyd.

It was to the south of the Priory that the Ogham stone was dug up in the 18th century and, according to a report in the *Cambrian Journal* of 1854, a farmworker on Caldey testified that a number of stone coffins had been found in the same area. There were many reports of bones being disturbed there over the years. The Ogham stone, before being moved eventually, and after many years, into the Priory chapel, had been used as a lintel for a window and then as a garden seat.

When Thornhill Timmins visited the island, c.1895, the Priory bell was still in position—'From the summit of the tower hangs the crazy bell, with rusty chain and silent clapper.' and the Ogham stone was then a 'recumbent oblong stone' in the 'dejected looking chapel.'

This, however, may more properly be left to a later chapter.

Having made occasional references to St Margaret's, what should perhaps be touched on here in the present context is the religious history of this little island.

By 1841 there were three houses on St Margaret's, and whatever building had been there previously had been converted. Not long before this, Fenton had observed at the time of his visit, 'St Margaret's, or Little Caldey, having the ruins of a large chapel, belonging to Lord Milford, as parcel of his manor of Manorbeer and Penaly, but generally rented of his lordship by the occupier of Caldey.'

St Margaret's Island, old chapel and cottage, with Dom Aiden O.S.B., 1919
(Photo: Tenby Museum)

A century and a half before that, the naturalist, John Ray, had written, 'This Island hath in it a small chapel, consecrated to St Margaret, from whom also the Island is denominated.'

Professor Rees, in his map of *South Wales and the border in the fourteenth century*, showed the island as Little Caldey and denoted that there was a chapel there. Saxton, in 1578, and Speed, in 1610, both showed the island, but without a name, whereas Lewis Morris, in 1748, gave it as St Margaret's.

In 1855, the *Tenby Observer* reported, 'A brass coin of Carausius has recently been found on St Margaret's island, which is particularly interesting, as Carausius was probably born at St David's. He was the commander of the Roman fleet, and having incurred the displeasure of the Emperors Diocletian and Maximilian, was ordered to be put to death; but feeling confident of the support of his fleet, he sailed over to Britain, and assumed the purple about A.D. 287.'

The finding of these coins is, of course, no indication that the Romans themselves were ever anywhere near the island. What was perhaps of rather more significance was the finding of bones and coins on nearby St Catherine's. The *Tenby Observer*, in 1868, reported that when excavating the site being built on St Catherine's, incidentally of blocks of granite being brought from Lundy, human bones had been found under the ruins of the chapel; also a few coins, one of which was dated 1161. One coin, of which an impression was sent to the British Museum, was declared to be a groat of Edward III, (1327-1377), in common use at the time.

There could originally have been a small anchorite's cell on St Margaret's, but the fact that Fenton refers to 'the ruins of a large chapel' is significant. And this brings us to the most significant reference of all.

Being neither scholar nor historian, but merely a scribe and seeker out of facts, I asked about the St Margaret to whom this chapel had been dedicated because I felt it was the sort of information which should be recorded. People I thought would know proved to be surprisingly vague on the subject.

In the end I went to the volumes of the *Catholic Directory of*

Saints to find out who St Margaret was, and there discovered that there were no fewer than eighteen of them, which was nothing if not giving a reasonable choice.

By a process of elimination it seemed as certain as can be that the dedication was to St Margaret of Antioch.

The *Penguin Dictionary of Saints* says, 'There are points of resemblance between the cultus of this Margaret and of Katherine of Alexandria; in the middle ages they were sometimes represented together.'

So that accounts for the twin chapels at either end of the great stretch of Tenby's south beach, St Margaret's and St Catherine's, and Tenby's annual fair has also been known as St Margaret's Fair since Elizabethan times and traces even further back.

In Butler's *Lives of the Saints*, it says of St Margaret, or Marina, Virgin and Martyr, 'On July 20th the Roman martyrology celebrates ''the passion at Antioch of the holy Margaret, virgin and martyr,'' formerly one of the most famous and widely venerated saints of the church.

'St Margaret's name appears in the Bosworth Psalter and other tenth-century English calendars and at the provincial council of Oxford in 1222 her feast, like that of St Catherine and some other saints, was made a holiday of obligation.'

Lastly, David H. Williams, in his very comprehensive new work, *Welsh Cistercians*, says, 'Neath possessed a holy well at St Margaret's chapel in Coed-ffranc. This, again, was a centre of pilgrimage which survived until recent times. As early as 1247, the abbot of Neath petitioned the General Chapter to allow the celebration of the feast of St Margaret in his abbey to ''more easily obtain the favour of his persecutors who hold that virgin in great devotion and veneration and have a chapel dedicated to her''.'

And at this point we can begin to look at the story from 1800 or so onwards.

Chapter 9

Cabot Kynaston

One of Thomas Kynaston's first acts after buying Caldey was to build the handsome mansion adjoining the old Priory. It contained seven major bedrooms and all the usual reception rooms. It is possible that his son Cabot, who followed him, also erected new farm buildings eventually, although the figures shown by the various *Census Returns* suggest that the Kynaston farming was not as intensive as that which came later.

From the agreement between Thomas Kynaston and David Llewellyn it is evident that the intention was to exploit the limestone. For many years limestone had been quarried on the South Pembrokeshire coast for burning and putting on the land. Now was also to come a time of tremendous quarrying of limestone for building purposes and road making. On Caldey there were four or five such old quarries but the Kynaston family also opened up and developed the High Cliff quarry from which eventually 20,000 tons of limestone a year were to be exported. It also seems that it was the young Cabot who was the driving force.

In 1804, for example, there is no mention of quarrying on Caldey in *Donovan's Excursions through South Wales.* 'Proceeding up the Island,' he wrote, 'we could not avoid observing it to be thinly inhabited, and so far as we went, at least, in a meagre state of cultivation . . . There are scarcely more than half a dozen houses on the island . . . Wild rabbits are everywhere abundant on this spot beyond conception—so numerous were they that the sale of their skins realized more than sufficient to pay half the yearly rental of the island.'

Could there be any connection between this statement of half the yearly rental being paid from the rabbit catch and the wording of the mortgage agreement between Thomas Kynaston and David Llewellyn?

The same statement was repeated in 1815 by William Rees in his *Beauties of Wales,* and it is not until on into the second decade of

The Priory mansion built by Thomas Kynaston, c.1800

Remains of Priory mansion, 1970

The state of the old Priory, c.1949

Repair work in 1950

the century that we find the beginning of the spectacular increase in the births of children to the labouring classes on Caldey as they were recorded in the church registers of Penally and Tenby.

Light is thrown on a number of these questions by a fascinating entry in the third diary in the National Library of Wales. It was kept by the Rev Sir Thomas Cullum and related to a journey into South Wales in 1811. He stayed at a Boarding House in Tenby for a fortnight in July that year and wrote, 'The expences for Board & Lodging are much the same as at Cheltenham, tho it at first appears less as you do not know all your expences here till the Bill is delivered as there are always a number of &c. &c.

'We have frequently made little excursions since we have been here. We took a boat the charge for which was 10s-6d. to the island of Caldey, which is well worth visiting as the Rocks on the further side of the island are very bold, & in some places quite perpendicular, & abound with an incredible number but apparently with no great variety of Sea Birds. We went with Mr Cooks who lives at Worcester and lodges in the House, he took his gun with him, and shot several Guls, Eligugs & Puffins, which with Sea Pies, seemed to constitute all the kinds this island seemed so much to abound with. The Chief production of the island is rabbits in the open country, but part is most expensively enclosed with very high walls and seems well cultivated, the remaining stock consisted of sheep and cattle, & we observed as many wheatears, as we had seen on Portland island, but no pains is here taken to catch them. The way the rabbits are caught is very simple, no nets or traps being used, they are caught by taking out the plugs at the bottom of the stone walls in the Evening & as the rabbits are sure to enter to feed upon the fresh Herbage, they then stop up the Holes, the rabbits are easily caught in the Enclosure. The Rocks are chiefly limestone from which a great profit is derived, but it is supposed that the owner Mr Kynaston, is loosing (*sic*) money by burning the Lime on the Island, instead of shipping off the Stone as was usually done. About 16 years since Mr K. bought the Island for £3,000, & has since been offered £10,000 for it but asks £12,000. There is a good House upon the Island, where Mr K. constantly resides.'

Thomas Kynaston had come to Caldey from Pembroke where, in 1789, he had purchased the property known as the Royal George, together with the quayside, for £400. He retained this property, better known in recent years as 'Jock's Bar', until 1810, when he sold it to a George Hurlow for £1,000. He profited that far by the inflated prices of the post-war boom, by which time Caldey also seems to have more than trebled in value from what he paid for it. He did not live to see the crash.

The reference to the burning of lime for sale is of great interest, because it influences any thinking there may be towards the idea that the lime-kilns were used to burn lime only for the land or for mortar in building. There may, however, have been some reasonable basis for Kynaston's thinking. Dr J. Geraint Jenkins says in his book, *Maritime Heritage*, in a chapter dealing with the trading pattern round the Cardigan coast and the practice of liming the land, 'Limestone was obtained from South Pembrokeshire including Caldey Island and from the Gower Peninsula and considerably more labour was required both to load and discharge limestone than handling culm.' It could just be that Kynaston found a readier demand for the burnt lime than the limestone.

To go ahead of the story, there are figures available for 1877, when Dr Jenkins quotes the cost of transporting lime (probably limestone) from Caldey to Aberporth on the coastal trader, *Elizabeth Ann*. A 'Prime Cost Cargo' was priced at £5-0s.-4d. Five days earlier the same vessel took a 'Prime cost cargo 56 tons @ 1/4 per ton, £3-14s.-8d.' from Lydstep.

The anthracite for burning the limestone in Thomas Kynaston's time would have been brought to the island by the same vessels that took the lime away.

When the new mansion was built at the Priory in 1800 it was a time of prosperity resulting from the high prices of the Napoleonic wars, coupled with a duty on imported corn. Corn could have been grown on Caldey, as it was on the other islands, without any immediate building programme, and we have the evidence of later writers that much good corn had been grown on the island. The inevitable recession came after the wars and, apart from the very occasional year, farmers suffered a bleak time from

1815 to 1853. The general gloom was deepened by a series of atrociously wet seasons.

There is mention in a schedule of 1799 of a 'lease and release between Thomas Kynaston and a Mary Levy of Pembroke, widow.' In 1800, her son, Samuel Levy, appeared in whatever transaction it was, along with others, including 'Thomas Makeig (of Scotland) in the parish of Llandegwed, Cardiganshire, mercer.' The Makeig family had long been active in trade in Cardiganshire, and it may not be idle to speculate as to whether Thomas Makeig had some financial interest in the development of the quarries on Caldey or, at any rate, the trade from them, possibly the burnt lime. There was a long history to the seafarers of the small ports of Cardiganshire.

Thomas Kynaston having died in 1812 or thereabouts, it would seem that young Cabot then began to show his initiative. In 1815 one John Thomas was living on the island where he was employed as a mason, for his wife, Alice, had a daughter, Ann, in that year. They produced further children in 1817, 1821, 1823 and 1827 and all the time John was shown as a mason, which rather suggests that building was going on.

It was a time of horrendous poverty amongst the rural population, and there was little opportunity for anyone to seek work elsewhere, because of the system of parish relief, and a distinct lack of enthusiasm on the part of the authorities to admit newcomers as a further burden upon the parish. This did not apply on Caldey, which was extra parochial, and the developments there must have been a lifeline for those who were able to avail themselves of it.

It is indeed fascinating to look through such old records as are available and see how people settled on Caldey from villages all over the south of the county—Saundersfoot, Amroth, Marros, Llanteague, Carew, Begelly, Penally, Jeffreston, Manorbier, Angle, Lamphey and so on. The names are all there. And there were, in addition, those who went over to work and lodged there from week to week, which culminated in the erection of a new building, known as The Barracks, to house them.

That Cabot Kynaston was spending money at this time is made

evident by a deed of Sept. 4th, 1818, between him, '. . . Sarah Kynaston of Southampton, mother of Cabot Kynaston and widow of Thomas Kynaston, with receipt for these deeds and the release of this date, being a mortgage of £4,000 and interest signed by Mary Duncan for herself and the mortgagees.'

It has not been easy to establish the facts about Cabot Kynaston, and it has been a slow process. The Registrars' Records go back only to 1837. Cabot Kynaston died in 1866 at the age of seventy-four. That means he would have been born about 1792. The 1841 *Census Returns* show him as being forty-five years of age, but the instructions to enumerators for that Census were to round ages, for those over fifteen years of age, down to the next five. They did not by any means always follow these instructions, but Cabot, at forty-nine, was correctly entered as forty-five, along with his family and household.

Of any early marriage I have failed to find a single trace, but the Penally church burial register has an entry on May 2nd, 1840, for 'William Kynaston, son of Cabitt Kynaston, Caldey, Gentleman.' William was seventeen years of age, had died of consumption, and the information had been given by Thomas Webb, who made his mark, and who has already been mentioned with his family as providing lodgings for the school mistress. Pembrokeshire people will know how he would have pronounced the name Cabot and why, therefore, the spelling appeared as it did.

William, therefore, must have been born about 1823, although there is no entry for his birth in either the Tenby or Penally registers. There is, however, one other significant entry and that is for the death of Sarah Kynaston on Caldey, in January 1827, at the age of forty-two. Cabot would then have been thirty-five and, for reasons which we can consider later, it seems that she was quite possibly his wife. To add to the confusion, his mother's name was also Sarah.

It is on these occasional church register entries that we have to depend to build up some sort of picture of what was happening. We know, for example, that in the 1841 *Census Returns* three families were shown as living on St Margaret's, and that by 1851 the island had been abandoned.

The first church register entry for St Margaret's was the death of Jane Cole at the age of forty-two in January 1834. So that it was some time, perhaps not very long, before that, that the quarrying on St Margaret's began in earnest, with the help of some of the £4,000 mortgage, and that the living accommodation was built there. In July of the same year, 1834, Julius Palmer, aged sixteen, died. He was the son of John and Anna Palmer. Two months later, in September, they had another boy and they christened him Julius, no doubt to replace the one they had lost—'The Lord gave and the Lord hath taken away. Blessed be the name of the Lord.' The registers show many instances of such happenings.

The next two births were in 1836 and '37, with a girl and a boy for George and Martha Rudd, who had married in Tenby in 1835. They had left St Margaret's by the time of the 1841 *Census*, when six of the total population of twenty-two people were quarrymen sharing the same billet.

The last entry was for the birth of a boy to a young couple, John and Mary Edwards, in 1842. From which we can perhaps put the occupation of St Margaret's at something like ten to twenty years. Kynaston must have had some sort of lease from Lord Milford, but so far I have not been able to find any record of such a lease in the *Picton Castle* or *Slebech Papers*. The task is not made any easier by virtue of Caldey's extra-parochial status.

One small reference of interest which I did manage to find, however, was in the Haverfordwest Gaol Register. On May 3rd, 1839, one John Davies, late of St Margaret's Island, entered into contract with John Beddows of Penally, a quarryman, until the first day of September. By July 15th the said John Davies would seem to have had enough of it, for he did absent himself from the aforesaid St Margaret's Island six weeks before the expiration of the term of the said contract 'and did then and there neglect to fulfil his contract.'

He was sent to Haverfordwest gaol, euphemistically referred to as a house of correction, to be kept to hard labour for one month.

The *Census Returns* show that a John Beddow was one of the quarrymen living on St Margaret's in 1841, and he could have been working on some sort of sub-contract system which was quite usual at the time.

Between 1811 and 1896 there were no fewer than one hundred and forty six children entered in the two church registers as having been born on Caldey. Apart from the notable exception of one young lady's contribution, of which more in a moment, only two of those were born out of wedlock, and in one of those two cases the parents subsequently married. It is quite a remarkable morality record compared with figures for the rest of the country at that time.

To return, then, to the notable exception. Slowly, one entry at a time, the list began to grow, until, for July 17th, 1814, I found the entry—Martha—illegitimate daughter of Martha Jenkins, Caldey Island. Neither name was unusual so I wondered vaguely who Martha might have been, and passed on. It is the sort of thing that can happen to the best of us.

For September 24th, 1815, however, there was another entry— Jessy, Natural daughter of Martha Jenkins of Caldey Island. With the best will in the world I could not help but be reminded of the old Pembrokeshire saying, 'If they haves thee once, shame on them. If they haves thee twice, shame on thee.'

The entry for Feb. 9th, 1817, was—Elizabeth, Natural daughter of Martha Jenkins, Caldey Island. Remembering the awful poverty of the age, the thought next occurred that somebody must have been providing for her.

Without going into any great detail, it is well to remember that before the *Poor Law Amendment Act* of 1834, where an unmarried mother claimed that a particular man was the father of her child, the onus was on the man to prove otherwise if he wished to deny parentage. If the mother on oath charged a man with paternity, a magistrate could commit him until he gave security either to maintain the child or to appear at quarter sessions to dispute the fact. Hence it is not at all unusual in church registers of the day to see such entries as Reputed Father, Claimed child of, and so on.

The law, however, was soon to be changed with a vengeance, and with the onus now being placed on an often helpless girl to prove parentage. The attitude of the day can be seen in the case of the one other entry for an illegitimate child on Caldey. In the margin, the vicar of Penally, God rest his compassionate soul, had written, 'No parishioner of mine.' In the St David's church register for the same period, there is eloquent testimony to the feelings of the clergyman who had charge of the entries in that parish of the cathedral city. The venom screams from the page of every entry as he dug in the great, sprawling word, Bastard!

In the case of Martha Jenkins there was no entry concerning the father, so presumably the issue was not in doubt. Then, two years later, for May 10th, 1819, came the fourth of her children—Mary— and the words 'Reputed daughter of Cabot and Martha Jenkins.' The words 'Cabot and' had been crossed off, to leave Martha on her own. Again it was for Caldey.

Her next child was Lucy, born on Oct. 31st, 1820, but this time Martha was given as of 'Town of Tenby'.

Then, on Jan. 18th, 1822, came Anna Maria—Illegitimate daughter of Martha Jenkins, Caldey Island.

All of this came as something of a surprise, for I had already seen the 1841 *Census Returns*. Martha, aged forty-five, is shown there as Kynaston, as are the girls, Martha, Jessy, Betsy (Elizabeth), Mary, Lucy and Anna Maria, and their ages all correspond with those of Martha Jenkins' children.

Anna Maria was born about a year before William, Kynaston's son, presumably by his wife, Sarah. We shall probably never know the real story, but it rather looks as if there was some impediment to prevent Cabot and Martha marrying, and that he married her eventually when he was free to do so, possibly after Sarah had died in 1827. What need to 'add a little romance'?

There are, however, one or two more points of interest. For Sept. 8th, 1832, there is another entry—Catharine—Illegitimate daughter of Martha Jenkins of Caldey Island, but this entry could have applied to Martha's eldest daughter of the same name who was by now eighteen years of age. Catharine died when she was seven months old.

The fact that the girls did take Kynaston's name is quite clear. Amongst the people in his household for the 1841 Census was a man by the name of Samuel Bryant, aged thirty-nine, and a surgeon. That Census was taken on June 5th. So, who was he?

The answer is provided by the Penally church marriage register which shows that, on June 8th, he married Jessy Kynaston of Caldey, in the presence of her father, Cabot Kynaston, Gentleman. Samuel Bryant was shown as a widower of Bristol.

Four years later Lucy married William Bird Herapath, also a surgeon, and also of Bristol. And the following year Anna Maria married Andrew Steven Reed, Esquire, of Tenby. In each case it was in the presence of their father, Cabot Kynaston, Gentleman.

William Bird Herapath became a brilliant scientist, an F.R.S., who had a mineral named after him, and also a street in Bristol.

So, the girls married well, as the saying goes, and had obviously been educated, for, in an age when so many made their mark, they signed the register in a neat hand.

Light was shed at last, after much tedious research, by the discovery of two more references. The first was for the death of Martha Kynaston, which suggested that Cabot had eventually married her, and which renewed the enthusiasm to search for an entry for the marriage. It was found at last in the church register for Manorbier where, on July 18th, 1833, 'Cabot Kynaston of Caldey Island in the County of Pembroke and extra parochial, Esquire, and Martha Jenkins of the same place, Spinster, were married by licence'. The oldest of their six daughters, the younger Martha, was then nineteen. The youngest, Anna Maria, was eleven. So they would have been all right for bridesmaids.

The entry for Martha Kynaston's death turned up in Bristol where she died, at the age of fifty-seven, in June 1851, at the home of her son-in-law Sam Bryant. She died of chronic colitis and lobular pneumonia. For that reason, possibly having gone to Bristol to her daughter, Jessy, to be looked after whilst she was ill, and before pneumonia set in, she did not appear on the 1851 *Census Returns* for Caldey.

Would today's medical people, I wonder, suggest that the colitis was caused by some of the undoubted worries and disappointments of earlier years? In any case, it is good to learn that she died within the love of her family.

There are three other names in the Kynaston household for the 1841 Census which are worth mentioning. The first, following after Samuel Bryant, is Jno Keannials, aged eighty-five. That was probably not his name, but the writing is bad and faded. Three days later he signed his name, which is even less decipherable, in the Penally church register, in a shaky hand, as a witness at the wedding of Bryant to Jessy.

We also find Joseph Morgan, aged twenty-four, an agricultural labourer. Maria Lewis, at that time, was thirteen and living with her parents. Joseph had come from Laugharne. They were still there in 1871, by which time they were married, with a family, and Joseph was the farm bailiff.

The other noteworthy entry is William James, also an agricultural labourer, shown as thirty-five years of age. He came from Angle, lived and died a bachelor on the island, and was better known as 'Ned of Caldey.' He died in 1876, at the age of seventy-two, and will go down in history as the man who was able to give the early 19th century writers most of the information they were able to glean about the finding, and subsequent history, of the famous Caldey Ogham stone.

Done Bushell referred to 'Ned of Caldey' as having been an Edward James. Normally it would not have been a bad guess but, as it happens, there is not a single instance of an Edward James anywhere in the island records throughout the 19th century.

Chapter 10

'Melancholy Accident'

Reference has already been made to the unbelievable poverty which followed the Napoleonic wars throughout the first half of the century. Not least of the problems of the day was the system of parish relief. Where a man could not keep himself and family he could turn to the parish to make up the difference. Inevitably the employers, which usually, in rural areas, meant the farmers, kept the wages low, thereby throwing an extra burden on the rates to be collected for relief of the poor. Young people tended to marry, before ever they were in a position to do so financially, and bring children into the world to be supported by the parish.

In an attempt to break out of the pernicious system, the work-houses were built, and that made matters worse. The workhouses were for those who could not support themselves outside, and conditions in them were deliberately made so unspeakable as to discourage anyone from seeking solace therein. People would suffer untold hardship and poverty rather than resort to them willingly.

These were the conditions at the time when Cabot Kynaston developed the Caldey quarries. There was no parish relief on Caldey so, as the only employer, he paid a living wage. If there were any poor, he had to keep them himself and, from the occasional references of various writers, it is quite evident that he did so fairly. It would also have provided a strong incentive to those who lived and worked on the island to remain there.

The *Education Report* of 1847 had also said, 'Tithe and poor-rates are standing monuments, in the common and statute law, of what in this country has been considered due in the way of spiritual and physical maintenance from landed property to the creators of its produce. Both of these incidents, however, are connected with such property by virtue of its being parochial; Caldy is extra-parochial, and, accordingly, the labourers upon it have neither church nor settlement.'

Something of the poverty of the day may be gathered from a report of the terrible Caldey tragedy of Christmas 1834. It appeared in *The Welshman* on Friday, January 2nd, 1835.

Melancholy Accident—Fifteen persons drowned in crossing from Caldy Island to Tenby.

On Saturday, the 27th ult, it had blown a strong steady breeze from the east, and there was rather a heavy sea running, but not so much so as to cause any serious alarm, as the boat had left the island of Caldy and made the passage in much worse weather. The proprietor of the island, C. Kynaston, Esq, after paying the quarrymen and farm labourers employed on the island their wages, which amounted to about £13, advised them to wait until the wind had abated and the sea gone down; but they, anxious to get home to their wives and families, refused the advice, and thirteen men and two young women got into the boat and put to sea at about twenty minutes before four in the afternoon. It appears that some of them had their doubts as to the practicability of making the passage, as the man who usually manages the boat refused to venture, and another went on shore twice, but was eventually prevailed on to accompany them. The distance from Caldy Island to Tenby is about two miles and a half. They had been at sea about twenty minutes, and would have reached their destination in about five minutes more, when the boat, which had been observed the greater part of the time from the island as well as from Tenby, and appeared to labour much on nearing Scur Rocks, at the back of St Catharine's, where the tide runs very strong, broached to, shipped a heavy sea, and went down instantly. Six or eight persons were seen floating after the fatal sea had passed over them, but the succeeding one, which had immediately followed, hurried them all into eternity. A six-oared gig immediately put off to their assistance, but not a vestige of the boat or passengers was to be seen, and it is doubtful, had they been in company, if they could have rendered them any aid, the accident was so instantaneous. Saturday, being market day at Tenby, many of the wives and friends of the unfortunate men from the villages in the neighbourhood were waiting their arrival, and as soon as the alarm was given they hurried to the South Sands, near where the accident had occurred. Here the scenes of distress and lamentation which presented themselves may be conceived but cannot be described. This disastrous event has left seven widows, thirty-three children, and four aged relatives, who depended more or less on the unfortunate sufferers for support, and who have to deplore their melancholy loss. On visiting the room of one of the miserable widows, of the name of James, who has a family of eight children, a few days afterwards, she was lying on some straw, without a bed or even bedclothes to cover her, and in the greatest distress. One of the children stated that they had not a mouthful of bread, or the means to procure it, when the dreadful accident happened. In another instance, Joseph Lewis, who has left a widow and six children, had promised to bring home some barley, and get it ground the same evening, and when the boat went down, his wife was heating the oven for the purpose of baking it. The small bag of barley was the first thing washed on shore from the ill-fated boat. For several hours during low water the first night the South Sands as far as Giltar Point were thronged with persons carrying lights, anxious to recover the bodies; and some of the relatives have been watching every night since the dreadful catastrophe. Three of the bodies were picked up on Tuesday the 30th ult. and conveyed to the Town Hall, and three have since been found, upon all of whom inquests have been held, and verdicts returned of—Accidental Death. On the bodies already taken up £9-1s.-6d. has been found. A subscription will be entered into, and we hope these heart-rending particulars will not meet the eyes of the humane and benevolent in vain.

An important function of the local newspaper in those days, and for a long time to come, was to disseminate news from other parts of the country and from abroad. The next item to the report of the Caldey tragedy, quite by chance, gives another glance at rural conditions of the day.

At Taunton, on Saturday last, a farmer sold a sack of good flour, a hogshead of cider, and a flitch of dry bacon, of his own feeding, for £2-10s.; a few years ago the same articles would have fetched £6—we mean when rents and tithes were nearly as they are now. The farmers must be relieved by the tithe owner and landlord, or many of them will go to the workhouse before next Michaelmas.

The following week *The Welshman* reported:

Tenby—We are happy to state that the subscription for the relief of the unfortunate widows and children of the men who were drowned in passing between Caldy Island and Tenby on the 27th ult. is progressing rapidly, already £150 having been received. In this are included sums of five and ten pounds, which have been forwarded by post from real, although unknown, friends of the widow and fatherless. Out of the fifteen bodies only nine have been recovered; the last two or three were so much mutilated as scarcely to be recognized by their relatives.

A. L. Leach in his *Guide to Tenby*, published in 1898, referring to Penally, said:

> In the upper part of the church-yard a plain stone preserves the memory of some of the victims of a great disaster which overtook the Caldey boat, on a stormy day in Christmas week in 1834 . . .
>
> The memorial stone stands beneath the wall of the old school-house of the village, now the parish reading-room. Fifteen persons lost their lives, twelve men and three women. The boat had on board, besides her human freight, a quantity of grain for customers on the mainland.

That stone is no longer to be found, nor are there those who can remember seeing it. With the moving of old stones which takes place in churchyards from time to time this is not surprising. What is surprising is the lack of entries in the more likely church registers. I have only been able to find entries for four of those who could possibly have been drowned on that occasion.

In the Tenby register there is—Thomas James—Town—Dec. 31st 1834—age 40.

In the Penally register there are two—William Thomas—Tenby— Jan. 3rd 1835 age 37, and—Thomas Thomas—Tenby—Jan. 5th 1835 age 45.

And in the Lamphey register there is—Ann Williams—Tenby— Dec. 30th 1834 age 27.

There is a story, handed down in the James family of Caldey, but for which no written evidence can be found now, a century-and-a-half later, that two James brothers of Caldey were drowned on that occasion.

In a number of other parish registers for the surrounding area I found no entries of significance and cannot help but wonder whether some of the casualties were buried on Caldey in some sort of communal grave. Whose, I wonder, were the bones which were found by Fr Robert to which I made reference earlier. The more I have delved into the Caldey records the more convinced I have become that there could have been some sort of register for baptisms and deaths kept on the island, and which was discontinued after the monks of the day embraced the Roman Catholic faith in 1913. Even if such a book did not exist, it is evident that many baptisms and burials took place on the island. The service in each case would have been performed by a clergyman from Tenby or Penally. Human nature being what it is, some of the entries could have been overlooked on return to the mainland. Certainly not all those ceremonies entered in the Penally and Tenby registers actually took place in those churches. I know, for example, that my mother's eldest sister was baptised on the island, but the entry appears in the Tenby register.

It is unlikely, therefore, that we shall ever now be able to trace the identity of those who perished with the Caldey boat in 1834. Alan Thomas, who has been the Caldey boatman since 1970,

Skipper of the Caldey boat, Alan Thomas (right), with engineer, Ted Richards

comes from a family of vast ramifications who trace to way back before that time to a John Thomas who was born in 1742. Alan's father, William (Billy Ayla), was a seaman before him, as well as a distinguished centre threequarter in the powerful Tenby rugby team of the 1920s and 30s. In writing this I am glad to remember that, as a callow youth, I played one game in the centre alongside him. Ayla's father was another William and also a seaman. That William's father was a George Thomas who worked in the quarry on Caldey. There is no point in going into more detail. Suffice it to say that, between 1811 and 1835, of the Thomas children born on Caldey, four were christened George, four James, three Thomas and one William. A George would call his first son George and his next son John or James or Tom. They, in turn, would call their own sons by a permutation of these Christian names. Even the family cannot these days sort them all out as they divided up eventually into clans, each according to an original nickname such as Fatter, Troll, Puffin, Statch and Cutty.

Apart from the names already given it is known in the family that Mary Thomas, a grand-daughter of the original John Thomas, married a man Webb who was drowned on the Caldey boat in the 1834 tragedy. There is also a story in the family that the man's father had had a premonition that he would never see his son again.

In looking through the lists of the Thomas family one item is worth a passing mention. On June 8th, 1823, a boy Thomas Thomas, born to Thomas and Mary Thomas was baptised. On June 10th, his death at the age of three days is recorded. It would take a great deal to convince me that they would have taken that little mite all the way to Penally to have him baptised, or that they would have taken him back again two days later to bury him. Yet there he is in both mainland registers.

The Thomas family, for the most part, had left the island by the 1850s. In 1841 the John Thomas, mason, was still there, aged sixty, with his wife Alice and their three youngest children, and in the 1860s James and Margaret Thomas had two children there. If it is of any guidance to the researcher, the girl was christened Mary Ann and the boy Thomas.

George Thomas, c.1865. His sister Mary married a Webb who was lost in the Caldey boat disaster of 1834, and he found the body of his own brother on the South Beach after the same disaster

To try to sort out the ramifications of the Webb family would be just as complicated. Then we have the other longstanding island family, the Rowes. George Rowe, quarryman, was there in 1841 and again in 1851, when George was sixty and his wife, Jane, was sixty-seven. Amongst their children they had two sons, David and George, born in 1818 and 1821. In due season young George grew up and married. His mother's name was Jane and she came from Williamston, near Carew. So young George marries another Jane, also from Williamston. He went one better than his father, however, because, whereas the older George took to himself a wife seven years older than himself, the young George married a Jane who was thirteen years older than he was. David also married a Jane, but there is no indication as to her age or place of origin, but when their son was born they called him George. The original young George was still on the island in 1881 working as a quarryman, and his wife Jane, now shown as seventy-three and fifteen years older than George, was working as a laundress. His mother had still been on the island in 1871 at the age of ninety.

In between times a Rowe would marry a Webb or a Thomas and the confused picture is completed. Not that it needs many members of a family all with the same names to cause confusion. The 1871 *Census Returns* show a quarryman by the name of John Jobe, aged forty-five, with his wife, Sarah, aged thirty-six, and their son James, aged six. John was given as from Llanddowror, Carmarthenshire, as was Sarah, and their son, James, as having been born in Narberth. In 1881 John Job is given as having come from Ludchurch, which is not all that far from Llanddowror, James is now fifteen and still from Narberth, whilst Sarah, who is still from Llanddowror, is now seventy-four. If that is correct she had young James when she was about fifty-nine and should have appeared in the *Guinness Book of Records* long ago.

The first thought is that the seventy-four, in figures, could have been a badly written forty-four, although it did not appear so. And, in due course, Sarah appears in the burial lists as having died on Caldey in 1901 at the age of ninety-six. Could it have been that the first Sarah died and that John married again to another Sarah twenty years older than himself?

Now Job at that time seems to have been a singularly singular name, for, search the relevant registers as we may, there is not a sign of a single Job, born, buried or married, anywhere to be found. Except, that is, for Caldey, where else, more than twenty years earlier, where it is recorded amongst the births—James Job—March 10th, 1858—Male—3 minutes—Son of John Job of Caldy Island—a stone quarrier—Weakling—No medical attendant.

And poor John Job, who was present at the death, made his mark.

Even at this distance of time can we not pause in passing to spare a thought for their distress and helplessness in the ignorance and squalor and bleak poverty of the day?

In such a pause for reflection we might even be better able to understand the anxiety of those who urged the boatmen to take

the ill-fated boat across just after Christmas in 1834. We know
how persuasive we can sometimes try to be ourselves. How much
more pressing would have been the sense of urgency for the poor
man with his bag of barley meal, knowing that his hungry family
were waiting for him and depending on him?

Chapter 11

Visitors and customs

In 1841, Kynaston was employing five agricultural labourers and the number was again the same in 1851. It suggests something of the close-knit nature of the community when it is realised that four of those in 1851 had also been there ten years earlier. The fifth, Joseph James, had also been there in 1841 in another capacity. He was of the family from which two brothers had been drowned seven years earlier. His first wife, Mary, died in 1846. According to the countryman's way of thinking it must have been a happy marriage, for the following year, at the age of thirty-six, he married a girl of twenty-one, Sarah Davies, formerly of Llan- glydwen, who had gone to Caldey as a servant. They were still on Caldey in 1864 when Sarah had, presumably the last of her six children, Martha. Would I be accused of being an incurable romantic if I were to suggest that God knew his business when Sarah went there in the first place? And this is not the last we hear of the family on Caldey.

The number of workers employed suggests that the farming was just about average. It was the farming which was to come later in the century which was to prove to be exceptional.

Writing in 1843, Mary Anne Bourne had written, 'A great part of the island is in a high state of cultivation and very productive.' And that, be it remembered, was at a time when farming fortunes were still at quite a low ebb. It was from 1850 onwards that things began to improve.

It was also round about that time that one of the island stories had its origin. What seems to be the most reliable version I have been able to find was in the May edition of *Pax* in 1920. Writing of the weather of that time, the contributor said:

> There has been nothing comparable to the experience which befell the father of John Lewis, the kind old carrier, to whom many of our visitors are indebted for catching their train at Tenby station with luggage intact. Seventy years ago, Mr Lewis was one of fifty men from the mainland who were working on Caldey, in the days of Mr Roger

Kynaston. The gales sprang up, and rough weather set in, and for five whole weeks they were marooned on the Island, unable to get away. By the end of that time they were reduced to eating mussels and limpets, gathered from the rocks below high-water mark: and Lewis was five weeks old before his father saw him.

The reference to Roger Kynaston means nothing at all. Where the name first appeared I have not been able to ascertain, but a number of the devotees to the secondary sources have cottoned on to it over the years, and it still appears from time to time. On the other hand, it must be acknowledged that, in the affidavit to the lawsuit in 1833, George Llewellyn referred to Thomas Kynaston and his sons, but I have found nothing to indicate that there was any Roger involved.

The only John Lewis I can find in the birth registers was born in August 1850 and, where newspaper reports of the day referred to the weather at that time, it would seem to have been very good. John Lewis, the carrier referred to, also known as 'John Trickle', died on March 18th, 1929, and was buried at Bethesda Chapel. The chapel register gives his age as eighty. So the reference in the *Pax* item in 1920 to 'seventy years ago' would seem to be reasonably accurate. Nowhere so far, however, have I been able to find any newspaper report which refers to such a happening round about the date of his birth.

Earlier I quoted what Fanny Price Gwynne had to say in 1852 of the custom of the islanders in taking the eggs and young of the sea-birds. Of Cabot Kynaston, she wrote, 'His character of unbounded hospitality, politeness and kindness, as well to the stranger as the friend, is so well known as to have been long since proverbial; and thousands who, though strangers, have been partakers of his hospitality, can with me bear witness, that there does not exist a more kind and amiable person than the present owner of the island.'

She, too, wrote of 'the very productive arable, meadow and pasture land.'

A particularly pertinent reference of Mrs Gwynne's, however, is where she writes, 'The produce is readily sold on the island, saving the trouble of water carriage to Tenby, as the noted Caldey roadstead is always frequented by vessels of large burthen, being the safest anchorage in the Bristol Channel during storms; two hundred sail can ride at anchor here.'

Towards the end of that same decade, in 1858, Mason, in *Tales and Traditions of Tenby,* said:

> Of all the holiday seasons kept by the inhabitants of Tenby, the most interesting was the 'Maying time' . . . Large parties were in the habit of visiting Caldey Island, there to pass away their time with rabbit and puffin shooting, and pic-nics on the beach. As the entertainments were not governed by the laws of temperance, the boatmen were not always in a fit condition to take charge of those who had committed themselves to their care. Hair-breadth escapes from a watery grave were very frequently experienced.

These visitations say something for the geniality of Cabot Kynaston to have permitted this sort of thing. And, at this juncture, we can call to mind again the fact that, although the schoolmistress had been drowned shortly before the visit of the Commissioners enquiring into the state of education in 1847, and they were accordingly critical of the lack of schooling at that time, by the time Mrs Gwynne was writing five years later a school was again in being.

An example of the horse-play to which Mason was referring is to be found a few years later in a report in *Potters Electric News* on June 5th, 1861—'Henry Cole Bowen charged with having on 20th May 1861, at the island of Caldey, feloniously with a certain gun, then and there loaded with gunpowder and divers leaden shot, shot at and against John Noot . . .'

Noot had been in a boat with T. A. Jenkins, T. Davies, T. S. Phillips and T. Lewis on the Whit Monday.

No witnesses came forward and there was a suggestion that the complainant had been bought off. Then one witness was called but would not answer.

'The Mayor cautioned Mr Bowen against in future getting excited, and said the parties had not behaved as they ought to have done in taking out a warrant in such a serious case, and then neglecting to appear.

'The case was then dismissed and the complainant ordered to pay costs.'

It was about this time that Dix had referred to the slaughter of the puffins on Whit Monday and had added, 'It is as much an institution as May Day with the sweeps.'

Writing in the 1890s Murray Mathew expressed the hope that the recently enacted Wild Birds' Protection Act would have put a stop to the cruel custom. It did. But it was not much help to the puffins, because the age of oil pollution had already been ushered in, albeit unsuspected and unheralded, and the puffin population, along with that of the other sea-birds, has been declining ever since.

There was one other pastime in which islanders and others would have indulged, and that was the killing of the seals which came, as they still come, to the island's caves to breed. I have not found any reference to the practice on Caldey, but there are ample references to its having happened on the other islands of Skomer and Ramsey, and it is as certain as these things can be that the custom on Caldey would have been the same.

We are further indebted to Mrs Gwynne for details of the Kynaston establishment at that time. She wrote of a 'plantation beside the lawn,' and 'two luxuriant flower gardens, well stocked with choice flowers,' as well as 'two fish-ponds, well stocked with choice fish, close to the house.' In an age when the rich were rich and the poor were poor, there were 'two large and very productive gardens, well stocked with fruit and vegetables; and under an enclosed building, is a never-failing spring of the purest water, which fills the farm-yard pond, two fish ponds, and turns a corn grist mill near the house, afterwards forming a pond near the cottages on the beach.'

The corn mill was still working, and the cottages were still on the beach, so that the sand had not yet accumulated in Priory Bay to form what eventually became known as The Common.

A decade later, in 1861, we have further useful insight into life on Caldey at that time with the publication of *Tenby: Its History, Antiquities, Scenery, Traditions and Customs*, by Mr & Mrs S. C. Hall.

Having made the usual references to the Whitsun visitations and puffin shooting, the Halls went on:

> Fern, which grows in abundance on the island, is gathered by the inhabitants, stacked, and serves for fuel, for thatching, and for litter; it also supplies the public oven, which is attended to, for a week at a time, by each of the housewives in turn.
>
> On market days the boat comes over to the mainland, and returns laden with whatever is required by the inhabitants for the week. As the stormy season advances, however, there is need to store up a more complete supply, as, from the violence of the sea, the communication is sometimes stopped for weeks together.
>
> There is excellent fishing around the island; the oyster fishery, indeed is renowned. The beds, at present not sufficiently worked, supply those fish that, taking their name from the nearest town, are welcomed everywhere on account of their size and delicate flavour. It is of these oysters the old Lord of Kemes (George Owen), in the reign of Elizabeth, says, 'there is a greate kinde gathered there, which, being eaten rawe, seeme too strong a meate for weak stomaks, and must be parted in two, three or foure peeces before he may be eaten, by reason of his exceeding bigness.'

If the Halls thought that the oyster beds were being underworked it was because the oysters were declining in numbers. By the beginning of the 19th century there had been warnings that the oysters were being over-fished, and by the end of the century the beds had been worked out. There was also lobster fishing.

The two particularly interesting references the Halls make are to the communal oven and to the boat. The oven is still clearly to be seen in the old Priory buildings. It is interesting that fern was used for heating. Fern, in this case, is what most people today might refer to more usually as bracken. It is also likely that sticks of the furze or gorse, and sometimes known as grunacks, would also have been used for heating. The significance of this will be appreciated from the reference in the tenancy agreement of 1771.

Water, too, was on something of a communal basis. What is now no more than an alcove in the village, near the village pond, was once known as the pump-house. There the village women went to draw water and have a chat. Nowadays the alcove houses a little statue of the Blessed Virgin, and one of the village ladies always ensures that there are fresh flowers there. It is many years since the pump was taken away, but the pipes at the back came to light again recently when the new shop was being built.

The reference to the boat is also of interest, because it establishes quite clearly that it was at that time based at Caldey, whereas it is now kept at Tenby, as it has been for the most part throughout the present century. It is a fact which suggests that there was still good harbourage in Priory Bay even up to the time of which the Halls were writing.

In an earlier chapter mention was made of the steps which had at one time existed where the boat landed near the old lime-kiln. This kiln was the one on the east side of Priory Bay and, for a time, it saw service as a boat-house. In some of the older estate maps a quay is shown at this spot, and it was only later that the present jetty was fashioned and a new road made. The brochure when the island was sold in 1897 said, 'A Pier or Jetty has recently been made at Priory Bay with a new road to it.' It is only when we remember this that we can make sense of the writings of earlier visitors to the island as they describe the road they walked from the beach to the Priory.

To revert to Cabot Kynaston, however, 'County Magistrate, Farmer,' according to the 1851 *Census Returns*, '10 Labourers. 16 Quarrymen.'

The quarrymen are all accounted for, bar one, in the Census, and the ten labourers consisted of eight masons, one carpenter, and a blacksmith. All, except the carpenter, were lodgers. So building was going on, and we call to mind that farming fortunes had taken a turn for the better and were to continue prosperous for another thirty years or so. It was very much in keeping with the times and with what was happening on the other islands. The fine farm buildings on Skomer were built in the 1840s.

Where, though, are the fifty quarrymen marooned in the storm? Presumably returned with the figures for the mainland where they lived, and they were paid on piece-work. The *Education Report* of 1847 had given the wages. 'The labourers (agricultural) earn 1s.-2d. or 1s.-4d. per day, with barley sold to them at 3s.-6d. per bushel, on their own finding. The quarrymen work by task, and taking the year round earn from 2s. to 2s.-6d. per day. They work, however, especially in summer, when the lime-stone is lading, a greater number of hours than common day-labourers. They draw their wages at the rate of 1s. per day, and receive the residue at the end of the year in one sum.'

In the *Pembrokeshire Herald* of March 18th, 1859, we find another interesting report:

> The proprietor of the beautiful and well-known island of Caldy, C. Kynaston, Esq, entertained with his accustomed liberality, the children belonging to the Island, in number about 40. After the tea and cakes had been disposed of with the zest peculiar to children, towards evening the parents of the children were regaled with cakes and ale. The bodily wants being thus satisfied, Mr Kynaston addressed them in a neat and feeling speech, pointing out to the children the benefits of a good, solid scriptural education, and showing that in the present day a knowledge of the rudiments of learning was absolutely indispensable for almost the most unskilled labour, and contrasting the advantages of an educated over an uneducated man, even if occupying the same position. On the parents he urged the necessity of their keeping their children to school, as long as they were able to do so; and impressed upon them the duty of showing a good example to their children, which would enable them to become useful members of society, and a blessing to themselves. The meeting broke up highly delighted with the entertainment, and giving three cheers for the governor and his lady.

This does not read like a man who discouraged, or was indifferent to learning. Nor does it seem to be referring to a man indifferent to spiritual values. The 1847 *Education Report* had said that he would not allow Dissenters the use of the church building. The more enlightened nowadays would think this hard, but perhaps we have forgotten that until 1828 Dissenters and Catholics had been lumped together insofar as they had been disqualified from being officials or members of public bodies. I wonder does the occasional ranting anti-Catholic nonconformist minister of today, and it is good to know they grow fewer all the time, ever pause in the midst of his blinkered and bigoted tirades to remember that we were both once regarded as social pariahs on the same footing?

The *Education Report* had also said, 'The proprietor does not permit a public-house to be erected on the island. The inhabitants, however, are rather out of the way of temptation than superior to it, whenever liquor can be had, either from vessels that are loading, or on their visits to the mainland.' In which case the proprietor should perhaps have been commended for keeping the workers and temptation as far apart as possible. Small wonder that he was often referred to as the King of Caldey.

Lastly, though, an interesting reference in the report of the island party is to the 'three cheers for the governor and his lady.' Who, in 1859, was the governor's lady? It was not Martha. No wife had been shown in the 1851 Census, for reasons we have already seen, although his daughter Martha was still living there, unmarried and thirty-six years of age. The registers say it was Rose Ellen Kynaston, who died six months or so later, on Oct. 17th, 1859, at the age of forty-eight, which would have been about nineteen years younger than her husband.

As proved to be the case with Martha, to find out more we again have to go to Bristol. In January 1852, seven months after Martha's death, Cabot Kynaston of Caldey Island married a widow, Rose Ellen D'Estelle Burjess, at All Saints, Bristol. Her father, Abraham Meredith, was a merchant. And the witnesses were Samuel and Jessy Bryant. So the family relationship seems to have been a good one.

The Bristol connection is interesting. Two of the Kynaston girls had married doctors from Bristol. How they came to meet in the first place may never be known, but Bristol was of great importance in communications with Pembrokeshire in the years before the coming of the railway. Before that the alternative was the stage-coach, and there are interesting references to this aspect of travel in the letters of John Henry, later to become Cardinal, Newman.

In 1846, the year after his conversion, Newman travelled from Gloucester to Tenby to visit his mentally sick brother. Amongst other things he wanted to reassure him that because he had become a Roman Catholic he had not become inhuman.

At that time there was a steamer service twice a week from Bristol to Tenby. The crossing, which on the occasion of Newman's journey was rough, took more than twelve hours. Even so, it was preferable to the return journey two days later. He left Tenby by stage-coach at 4.00 a.m. to catch the mail at Carmarthen. Presumably that would have been the old Cambrian stage-coach. He reached Gloucester at 11.15 that night. 'One step enough for me.'

In addition to the steamer service to Tenby there was also the coastal trade of sailing ships between Bristol and Tenby, with considerable sea trade with Caldey itself.

Cabot Kynaston died just before Christmas 1866, seven years after the death of Rose Ellen. *Potters Electric News*, of Jan. 2nd, 1867, reported the event briefly:

> Mr Kynaston's funeral took place on Saturday week, at the Tenby cemetry. It was followed by his sons-in-law, Dr Herepath, Bristol, Dr Bryant, Bristol and A. S. Read, Esq, Tenby, a large number of friends, and all the inhabitants of Caldey (of which island Mr Kynaston was the owner), amongst whom must not be forgotten William James, better known as 'Ned of Caldey'. This faithful servant has been in the service of Mr Kynaston and his father on Caldey, for 45 years.

The faithful William stayed on at Caldey for ten years or so with the new owner, James Taylor Hawksley. He went to his last long rest at seventy-two years of age in January 1876, and he had become sufficient of a legend in his own lifetime to warrant a special mention in the *Pembrokeshire Herald*, which said of him:

> Death has removed an old familiar face from among us. William James, better known as Ned of Caldey, was buried in the cemetery, Tenby, on Tuesday last. The greater portion of his life was passed in the service of the late Cabot Kynaston, Esq. of Caldey Island, as boatman, servant of all work, general messenger, to whose memory was entrusted commissions for supplying all requirements, varying from a packet of pins, a yard of ribbon, to the largest articles of consumption, not only for his master's family, but also for the numerous cottagers resident on the island. The death of Mr Kynaston

was a grievous sorrow to his attached servant who, to the last moment, could not speak of his old master without shedding tears. He clung to the old place like a limpet to the rock, and the purchaser of the island, J. T. Hawksley, Esq, retained him in his service for life. In his younger days Ned indulged too frequently in a friendly glass, though his arduous struggles through the stormy seas, at all hours, in all weathers, may have offered a better excuse than most other drinkers could have advanced in extenuation. For very many years Ned had continued a consistent and strict 'total abstainer'. He also endeavoured by every means in his power to persuade others of the evils of intemperance, and walked many miles to publickly address assemblages of working men on the duty of sobriety, fearlessly in his untutored language telling them of his own experience as to the sin of drinking to excess. It may truly be said of him that he was a man who tried to do his duty and did it. He died happy on Sunday, 23rd January.

As an ex-smoker I know how enthusiastically the convert can become 'anti'. St Paul is a rather more notable example. But it is good to read that Ned 'died happy.' His old friend, David Oriel, went over to the mainland to register the death at which he had been present.

The conveyance to Hawksley is in the Caldey archives and dated Nov. 25th, 1867. The sale price was £15,950. The contract was between Emma Mordaunt, spinster of Bournemouth, Martha Kynaston, spinster of Caldey and James Wilson Hawksley. He was the father of James Taylor Hawksley, a man of agricultural background, who came to farm the island for the next twenty-four years. He was the only son. The document says that Cabot Kynaston had made his will in December, 1865, in favour of John Bowers and Martha Kynaston. But John Bowers (a Tenby magistrate and old friend of Kynaston's), had died in 1867, whilst staying on Caldey, only three months after Kynaston had died and before the will was proved, so Martha Kynaston was the sole trustee. The will left the estate in trust to their heirs with instructions to sell after Kynaston's death. Clearly, this was done.

We find now, however, another of the unaccountable and insupportable statements with which writings of Caldey are strewn. Referring to the 'Caldey Reliquary' in his article in the

Archaeologia Cambrensis in 1870, three years after Hawksley had bought the island, Albert Way (thirty families in 1870!) said that the Reliquary belonged to 'Mr Edward Kynaston Bridger, the present possessor of the island . . .' Bridger, he said, was a cousin to Cabot Kynaston.

Surprisingly, A. L. Leach of all people, quoted this as fact in an article he wrote for the *Tenby and County News* in 1941, when he added the further interesting statement that Bridger allowed Done Bushell, because of his great interest, to retain the 'Reliquary' during his lifetime, and then Bridger's son, Hugh L. Bridger, wrote to the secretary of Tenby Museum on Oct. 18th, 1917, confirming that it was the family's wish that it should be a gift to Tenby Museum.

The 'Reliquary', found by Kynaston when he was digging out the wildcat, is in the shape of an altar tomb, eight inches long, and is surmounted by a recumbent figure. The probability is, in fact, that the lower part was originally the pedestal of a statuette and the recumbent figure an angel forming part of an alabaster representation of the Assumption of the Virgin.

Whilst the 'Reliquary' undoubtedly seemed to have passed to the Bridgers, the island did not. What particularly interests me, however, is the fact that the Bridgers were connected with the island at all, because, up to 1891, they were also frequent visitors to Skomer during the tenure of that island by Capt. Vaughan Palmer Davies. E. K. Bridger, of London, was a talented and prolific amateur painter in water colours, and many of his paintings are in the possession of the Davies family. His son, Hugh Bridger, was an engineer, based on Barrow in Furness. He died, unmarried, about 1950. He was a keen amateur photographer all his life and I am pleased to think that some of his splended pictures, taken on Skomer in the 1880s, appeared in my book *The Sounds Between*.

I wonder did Kynaston Bridger ever speak to my grandmother when she was in service on Skomer in the 1870s, and later in that decade when she had married and settled on Caldey. And did they, when she was on Caldey, exchange a few reminiscences about Skomer? I wonder.

Chapter 12

The Hawksley era

From here on, a wealth of material is available, and it becomes a question of knowing what to leave out.

Of the James Wilson Hawksley, who bought Caldey in 1867, I know nothing. It would seem that he bought it for his only son. The *Census Returns* say that the son, James Taylor Hawksley, was born in Birmingham. There was also a book, published privately in 1917, entitled *Lieut-Colonel John P. V. Hawksley, D.S.O., R.F.A.*, and written by his cousin, Margaret M. Verney. It gives some useful and interesting information about John's father, James T. Hawksley.

James T. Hawksley and his wife had four children whilst they were on Caldey. The two eldest boys went into the services and had distinguished careers. Then came a girl, Muriel Emily, followed by John, born in 1877. These two were very close in their relationship. John Hawksley also had a distinguished service career during the South African War, including the siege of Ladysmith, and then during the first World War until he was killed in the Battle of the Somme in 1916. He kept a diary, and it was on this and his various letters that the book was based. In it, his sister, Muriel Emily, who subsequently married a Robert Summerson, supplied a note on their lives as children on Caldey. She wrote:

We lived very healthy, outdoor lives, and had any amount of occupations and all sorts of sport, except hunting, which was not possible on the island, but we had our ponies. My father was at Shrewsbury School. The greatest reputation he gained there, I fancy, was the feat accomplished of sitting astride the weather-cock on the highest (or second highest) steeple in England. He had a scientific knowledge of farming, having studied at Cirencester; his farm at Caldy was a model and well known in South Wales. My dear father was a Liberal until Mr Gladstone brought in his Home Rule measure. This was a great blow to him, and although I was a child I noticed it; he felt he could not conscientiously follow. He refrained from voting at the next election and was a Liberal Unionist afterwards. He was a keen politician and I am told that he was asked to stand for the county, but I do not think he liked the fighting part of the business. He had a full life already and he dwelt among his own people. My mother's family were Conservative; my uncle Captain George Price, R.N., sat as a Member for Devenport for eighteen years.

My father never cared about a magistrate's work, although he sat on the bench when he could not avoid doing so; he had a very tender heart, and I am sure that the worst punishment for him was to inflict it. By far the greatest of all his interests was the training of his children. He was an ardent educationist in advance of his time, and looked into every detail of his children's lives with regard to the training of the youthful mind, even in the nursery.

He was adored by the working classes on Caldy and at Tenby also. Our old bailiff told me he had often been ordered to pay men their full wages for months and months, and for a year if they were unable to work, and no malingering was ever heard of; such things seemed impossible with the perfect trust and faith existing on each side. It was no weak good-nature on the master's side; his pluck was known to equal his kindness, and both appealed to his workmen. On one occasion when a tremendous gale was blowing and Caldy was cut off from the mainland, a woman in her hour of pain and peril urgently needed a doctor's help. Every man practically in the island could handle a boat, but we had then only open boats with a lugsail, and the bailiff came and told my father that no one would volunteer to cross the 2½ miles of angry seas. My father went out at once and explained to the men how urgent the case was, he said he would take a boat over himself, and asked if there was anyone who would help him. The woman's husband stepped forward, followed by his brother, then came another pair of brothers, both married men with large families; so my father started with these four men. He was himself at the helm, but the anxious population of Caldy who were watching, and others who caught sight of her on the opposite shore, never expected the boat to weather the storm; over and over again she was lost to sight, but she came into port. Then the wind abated with the turn of the tide, the doctor was brought over, and the woman's life saved.

My father died suddenly at Caldy on August 3rd, 1891, aged fifty-two. When the news reached the workmen in the limestone quarries (who were paid by tonnage), every man dropped his tools and went home. At his funeral they carried him half a mile themselves. Some years later I had been to see his grave at Tenby and found an old man there, who told me that he came to the cemetery once a week, and always went to have a look at the master's grave. 'He was such a good master he ought to have lived a hundred years.' I am sorry that Caldy had to be sold. It was a great grief to us and to the people; they would have liked my eldest brother to have lived with them, as they thought so much of him. Our mother was all that a mother ought to be. She was clever and capable, and had a wonderful mathematical mind. She was most business like when she had to manage the place for a few years after my father's death. The whole atmosphere of home depended on our excellent parents.

Randal and Jimmy, John and I, hunted in couples. The elder one had a tutor in the summer holidays to go about with. John and I were more with our governess, but sometimes we little ones were allowed to join forces with them as a great treat, in mild sports, such as catching prawns. John was not strong as a child and did not mind not being allowed to join in his brothers' more robust pursuits. It is strange to look back upon, when he has done and seen so much, that he did not care then to shoot, which I delighted in, and was allowed to practise if I could get someone to attend me. My governess struck at this, so our dear Nurse Davies was dragged out of her comfortable workroom, and put in a sheltered spot under a wall, where I also waited almost in the dark, for a shot at wild-duck which came over the island with a S.W. wind. John and our mother used to walk about together: I have them in my mind's eye going along, John's arm through hers in a companionable sort of way—he was very much mother's boy.

There was a real affection for Ann Davies, the nurse, who was to stay with the family throughout her life and was still with Mrs. Emily Hawksley when the latter died in 1906. Her daughter, Muriel, recalled another memory of their Caldey childhood:

The children had a pretty custom of making little nosegays for each of the servants to wear for going to church, but as Nurse Davies could never be persuaded to have a buttonhole, John used to put her flowers in her room, that she might find them when she got back.

There is so much in all this which helps us to understand something of what was happening on the island during the second half of the 19th century. Going to church was something of a special occasion which warranted a buttonhole, more so perhaps than if it had been a weekly occurence. And we can be quite sure that it was the village church of St. David's. We have already seen reference to the neglected state of the Priory at the time of H. Thornbill Timmins' visit, and this is more than amply borne out by the evidence of Done Bushell, who came towards the end of the century, and found that the sanctuary was a laundry (had not 'young' Jane Rowe been working there at the age of seventy-three in 1881?) the choir was a maltbin, lime was stored in the entrance porch, and the guest-house was a pigeon-loft. Many hundreds of bottles had been dumped in the narthex.

In addition to being a magistrate, Hawksley was High Sheriff in 1884, took an active interest in the civic affairs of Tenby, of which he was an alderman, and, for most of his time on Caldey, seems to have had a house in the town. When John was born in 1877 the family also had an address at 6, The Esplanade. In 1891, when Hawksley died, the coffin was brought across to his house at 3, North Cliff. When his widow died in 1906 she had a house at The Paragon. It was a time when houses to rent were readily available, as we are reminded when we look through the pages of the contemporary local newspapers.

From 1850 to 1880, farming prospered, so Hawksley, in 1867, had the misfortune to come in when prices were high. With his new scientific approach, and in the full, fresh vigour of young manhood, he possibly thought it would continue like that. Richard Jefferies, in *Hodge and His Masters*, written at that period, had much to say of the new thinking of the day. Hawksley had it all, including, in 1881, Amelia Bergerand, a French ladies' maid.

The farming was undoubtedly on a high plane, with Hawksley beginning as a foremost breeder of livestock and, by 1881, employing ten men and boys on the farm. In that year there were ninety-nine people on the island, with one cottage of the sixteen houses uninhabited and two people visiting elsewhere, so that the population actually just topped the hundred mark. One of them was a corn miller, William Oriel, from Llanteague. Nowadays they tend to spell it Llanteg, because, as far as possible in this land of ours everything must have a Welsh connotaton. But Llanteague it was originally, and 'teague' was the old Pembrokeshire word for the Irish in the days when many of that hard-pressed nation were itinerants looking for work hereabouts.

It seems, therefore, that the old mill was still working. Lodging with the farm bailiff, David Oriel, was the blacksmith, Owen Phillips of Saundersfoot. He had his blacksmith shop on the harbour at Saundersfoot when the colliery there was in its heyday. William Oriel was also shown as a lodger in the same house. He was probably David Oriel's uncle, being a cousin to David's father, Benjamin. Could the pair of them, blacksmith and miller, have gone across to carry out some repairs to the mill, or possibly to instal the new steam-driven mill for Hawksley?

There is no point in going into all the details of the various people involved but, in May 1876, Hawksley raised a mortgage of £10,000, and this would have been to finance the considerable building programme and other developments he had in hand and was contemplating. That mortgage was still in existence and transferred to a fresh party fifteen years later, just before Hawksley died.

A map in the Schedule attached to the mortgage gives some interesting details. Near the present jetty, by what was known, even then, as Rubbishy Corner, there had been an old quarry, and old quarry rails are shown. No doubt ketches had been beached nearby and the rails had carried the small quarry trucks. By this time, however, the terrain was changing, and it would have become more difficult to keep any sort of boat on the island. Certainly, by the 1890s, the documents show that the owners of Caldey had two moorings in Tenby Bay. By the early part of the present century there was a boat-house near this spot, with a tramway for pulling the boat up and down. It is reasonable to suppose that this would have been the old quarry tramway which had been adapted to a different use.

The two lime-kilns were shown, in the 1876 Schedule, to the east and west of Priory Bay respectively, there was a powder house shown near where the house known as Tŷ Gwyn now stands, and the old mediaeval round tower was also shown as a powder house. As a matter of interest to natives only, near what is now known as Den Point, there was shown Daniel's Den.

In the *Sale Brochure* of 1892 the 'obelisk' was indicated above Paul Jones' Bay. Nobody has ever been able to explain what this old building was. Older people once spoke of sheep having been gathered by a building near the cliff, and of shepherds sleeping there, but I have found no single mention anywhere to suggest what the function of this building really was. So the answer is, 'I do not know.' I would hate to think that some scribe, as yet unborn, could one day take this as a secondary source and say that Howells said this, or Howells said that, when Howells said nothing of the sort. I have more than enough of my own sins for which to answer on Judgement Day without having any made up for me by those who couldn't be bothered to do their own research!

Another building which has puzzled many is the remains of what looks like a stone silo above Red Berry Bay. Anyway, I always thought it looked like the remains of a stone silo, and it was something of a relief when I found that that was exactly what it was. It was clearly shown in the same brochure, marked number 44 on the plan, and the Schedule said, 'A large newly erected silo, stone built with corrugated iron roof.' I was glad to find this confirmation, because it not only gives me the chance to use long words like corrugated iron, but it is evidence of Hawksley's agricultural enterprise. To have been building that sort of silo at that time must mark him as something of a pioneer.

The chances are that it could have been about 1883, because that is the date carved into a beam of the great barn which was also probably built about that time. Hawksley could hardly have been expected to know it, but he was spending his money at a bad time, because agriculture had just entered a period of terrible depression. It had begun in 1879 after three successive rain-ruined harvests and was to culminate in the agricultural poverty of the 'Hungry Nineties'.

Before this he had carried out what was perhaps his most spectacular development with the building of vast greenhouses, and the installation of an advanced system of heating by steam. The water was pumped by a steam engine from the well house up to a tank at the high point of the island near the lighthouse, and from there it was fed back by gravitation to the gardens and farm. This equipment consisted of a 'horizontal boiler 10 H.P. and fittings, a vertical steam engine 6 H.P., and a vertical double action pumping engine for supplying the houses'. The waste steam, apart from being used to heat the greenhouses was also used to drive a 'threshing machine with open drain and fittings, a Vipon corn crusher, a Deaning cake mill, a Woodroffes root finger cut slicer, a turnip pulper and a Richmond and Chandlers chaff-cutter'. It is quite possible that the massive barn was built partly in order to house this great working collection of modern equipment. There was also a 'Wood & Co's corn mill for steam power' which possibly sounded the death knell for the old water mill.

The 'engine driver' at that time was John James, son of Joseph James, of whom mention was made earlier, by Joseph's young second wife, Sarah. There was another brother, Henry, and in due course, he took over as 'engineman'. Perhaps it would be as well to tell his story here.

Henry James feeding the kiln to produce lime for mortar during the building of the monastery

Henry James with his wife, Sarah and sister, Anne

Henry James married a girl named Ann Oriel. They had four children, and Ann died young. Then Henry married her sister, Sarah, and they, too, had four children. One of them was named Elizabeth, and her name will occur later on. So, who were Ann and Sarah Oriel?

They were the daughters of William Oriel, the miller, to whose presence on Caldey in 1881 we have just been referring. No doubt they were visiting their family on Caldey when Henry met them, for Caldey is a romantic place, and that is how these things happen.

In 1834 Benjamin Oriel, who is given in all the *Census Returns* as having been born at Marros, married a widow, Betsy Howel, eight years older than himself, from Llangining, and they settled in Llanteague or Crunwere, the adjoining parish to Marros. Llanteague is the hamlet and Crunwere is the parish. Their first two children were born there, and then, probably about 1839, they moved to Caldey.

Benjamin Oriel was a carpenter and would seem to have been a capable man who, in the tradition of islanders, could turn his hand to anything. He and his family lived in the end cottage of the row in the village which was one of those pulled down during the building programme carried out at the beginning of this century.

In due course he became Cabot Kynaston's right-hand man, and it was he who planted the fuschias which have remained as such a glory on Caldey ever since.

Benjamin and Betsy Oriel with their grand-daughter, Mary Ann

After more than thirty years Benjamin and Betsy left Caldey, not many years after Kynaston's death, and set up a grocery business at 6 Culver Park in Tenby. When Benjamin died in 1897, at the age of eighty-four, a newspaper report said of him, 'The sphere of his usefulness and vigorous labour was Caldey Island. There he laboured for forty years and exerted a marvellous influence over all who lived on the island. The inhabitants sought his advice in difficulties, his aid in disease and accident, and his mediation when disputes arose. He taught the children to read and write, conducted Sunday School and Services, and was looked up to by all as a kind of temporal as well as spiritual Father. He gained the high regard of Mr Kynaston by moral character and integrity that never stooped to deceit or sham. For many years he served as head gardener and was entrusted with general oversight in many matters.

"A man he was to all the Island dear,
And passing rich on forty pounds a year."

'The funeral service was conducted by his grandson, the Rev. B. Oriel, now the Baptist minister of a church near Bath. A small bow of blue ribbon was fastened on the coffin, and it was explained that no work was dearer to the departed than that of helping his friends to abstain from strong drink.'

Such a report gives rise to the legitimate speculation as to whether it was a grocer, and not a draper, as was suggested earlier, who used to go over to take the occasional service on the island. The blue ribbon would have been that of the old Band of Hope and we may well ask ourselves whether Ned of Caldey had been one of those whom Benjamin had converted.

As we saw earlier, Benjamin's daughter, Sarah, also became a schoolteacher on the island. She told her grand-daughter in later years that they held the school in the little church and that it was divided by a screen during the week for two classrooms and the screen was removed for the Sunday services. And they even held reading and writing classes for adults.

When James Hawksley came to the island in 1867 he brought with him a young man, John King, who had been his right-hand man on his farm at Navistock in Essex. John King lodged with

John King and Sarah Oriel when they married in 1872

Benjamin Oriel and, in 1872, married Benjamin's daughter, Sarah. To Hawksley's great disappointment the young couple did not stay on the island but went off to seek their fortune at Dowlais in industrial Glamorgan. Sarah already had a brother in business there as a tailor.

It was, as we have seen, Sarah's brother, David Oriel, who stayed on to become the farm bailiff, presumably succeeding Joseph Morgan.

After a time Hawksley had changed the emphasis of his farming enterprise from livestock breeding to market gardening, and developed between sixty and seventy acres of his land, possibly related to the enclosed area, for this purpose. There can be little doubt that he found the difficulties of crossing to the mainland with livestock militating against the success of such a business, just as it always has been, and always must be, a hazard for

David Oriel, farm bailiff for James Hawksley, with his wife, Martha

island farmers anywhere. It costs money and, when the extra bills have all been paid, the island farmer still only receives as much for his stock as the man on the mainland farm.

To carry the considerable bulk of produce from the market-gardens Hawksley had a seventy-five ton ketch, and she traded between the island and such places as Pembroke Dock and Swansea, as well as delivering to Tenby harbour.

One other point of interest is that we have a reliable record of the number of dwellings on the island at that time. In addition to the mansion there were 'thirteen cottages (nine in one block, one pair and two detached, one with thatched roof, the rest slated), each with garden; let by the year, to the labourers etc. on the Estate at rents amounting together to £33-16s per annum.' The rent of each cottage was a shilling per week. The cottage with the thatched roof was the one of which the remains can still be seen running out into the field just below the old mill and the ponds. I wonder was it the miller's cottage. I have seen an old picture of it, but doubt whether it is good enough to reproduce.

The family's era on Caldey effectively came to an end when James Taylor Hawksley died there suddenly on August 3rd, 1891. He had been unwell for some time but, during the week, had been visiting Tenby, returning to the island on the Thursday. The report of his death says, 'He was visited by Mr Beamish Hamilton on Friday, and some Tenby friends saw him on Saturday. He retired to his bedroom early on Sunday evening, and not coming down at his usual hour on Monday, his room was entered about noon by the farm bailiff, David Oriel, who found him dead.' So it would have been early on the Monday afternoon that the men in the quarry laid down their tools when the news came to them.

The story would seem to have been not an entirely happy one. David Oriel told one of his daughters later that the boss had taken his own life. James Hawksley experienced a good deal of disappointment because his wife spent little time on the island and was much more interested in the social round. Reference has already been made to the substantial houses being rented in Tenby and the style of the establishment maintained by the Hawksleys. A day or two before he died Hawksley was visited by

John King and he begged him to return to the island. John King always regretted that he had not stayed a few days and said, 'Perhaps then the tragedy might not have happened.'

Although the report does not say so, his widow would not appear to have been on the island at the time of his death. We know, however, from the extract quoted at the beginning of this chapter that she carried on for a time trying to run the business. She was about forty-five at the time and, even now, almost a century later, it is impossible not to feel for her. The semi-decade through which she struggled in the face of her hopeless task were years which are amongst the blackest ever recorded in the annals of British agriculture. As her daughter, Muriel, said in her memoir, the island 'had to be sold'.

The purchase price in the heady days of 1867 had been £15,950. In spite of the vast sums which had been expended on all kinds of improvements during the next quarter of a century, Caldey was sold in the spring of 1894 to Thomas Dick Smith-Cuninghame, for £12,750. It had been offered for sale in 1892, and I have no doubt that poor Emily Julia Hawksley was glad enough to cut her losses and get out. It marked the end of an epoch, and perhaps there was more than we can ever expect to understand in the heart of the old man who used to visit 'the master's grave' in Tenby cemetery.

Chapter 13

Island people

Of Thomas Dick Smith-Cuninghame there is little to be found in the records. He came from Lanark, in Scotland, and raised a mortgage of £5,500 from the Rev. Robert Wentworth Cracroft, Rector of Harrington, Lincoln, and the Rev. Charles Henry Fairfax, vicar of Hackthorne, out of 'monies belonging to them on a joint account', which at least suggests that the clergy were rather better off then than they are now. He had been educated at Harrow, but even that was not sufficient to enable him to survive in those times. If he needed to raise a mortgage, an off-shore island, in the 1890s, was the last place in the world to try to make the money to repay it. After only three years, he sold the island, on Dec. 21st, 1897, for £12,200 to the Rev William Done Bushell, which represented a capital loss of £550.

Cuninghame would seem to have been carrying on in something the same fashion as Hawksley, because the valuation included, for growing crops, £21 for parsnips and £19 for cabbage. I just wonder, however, what was happening in the quarries, because a brochure lauding the island when it was offered for sale, apart from referring to 'a small church and school house', and many other details with which we are now familiar, said, 'The nett Royalty now received from the Quarries is 6d per ton,' from which it would seem that Cuninghame was not working them himself.

The trade, by this time, was on the wane. I am not sure who it was who said that the only thing men ever learn from history, is that men never learn from history, but it would seem to be true. It is doubtful whether people have learned even yet that, without a prosperous agriculture, there can be no true national prosperity.

Another ominous reference in the same brochure was to the effect that 'Rabbits are very plentiful on the island, parts of which make fine warrens.' When a man is reduced to farming for rabbits, both he and farming must be in poor shape.

In spite of all this, Cuninghame's heart was obviously in the right place and, during his short time on the island, he went to the expense of thoroughly renovating the village church. It must have been the first thing he did, for the church was reopened on July 12th, 1894, with a Communion service, taken by Rev R. W. F. Davies, 'who preached an admirable sermon'.

There is evidence amongst the *John Francis Collection* of papers that the equipment in the schoolroom had been paid for with money subscribed by the islanders. Probably such enthusiasm was engendered by the work of refurbishing which had included a stove for heating, for the church and school were still in the same building.

Thornbill Timmins' book was published in 1895, so that his visit was possibly made shortly before the renovation of the village church, and he was therefore, in fact, referring to this when he wrote of the 'dejected looking chapel' and 'recumbent oblong stone', because the newspaper report of the reopening also went on to say, 'The ancient inscribed stone, which for some years was in the Church in a position that made it impossible to view it, has been fixed into the wall of the porch after being carefully cleaned.'

Another thing for which Cuninghame will go down in history, however, and certainly with those who have a feeling for the old days on Caldey, is the fact that it was he who introduced the well-known little steamer, *The Firefly*, to Tenby. Built at Aberystwyth, and named *Lizzie*, she was purchased by Cuninghame for island service in 1894, when she was ten years old. She was fifty-two feet long, with a displacement of twenty tons, and her twenty horse-power engines produced a speed of eight knots. For the next twenty-two years she served the changing communities faithfully until her greatly-mourned loss in a blizzard in 1916.

When Cuninghame sold to Done Bushell, in addition to *The Firefly* there was 'a lug sail boat, *May Queen*, 26'-6" long, beam 6', sails, spars etc.; a lug sail boat, *Governor*, length 21', beam 8'-9", with sails etc.; a five oared gig with oars and sails, a three oared punt, a pleasure dinghey and a punt for the lake.'

The *Inventory to the Valuation* runs to thirty-seven hand-written pages, and is marvellously evocative of an age which is past, with

The famous *Firefly*

its lists of butter-workers, pans, milking stools and other such equipment necessary to the proper management of the dairy, and it would provide the basis for a long essay.

There were seven horses and a pony, and they included Violet (aged), Boxer, Scott, Farmer and Darling (rising five years).

Amongst the fifty-four head of cattle there was a three year old Angus bull, and the Angus breed predominated (had not the boss man come from Scotland?), but there were also a Jersey cow, a white cow, a blue cow and a strawberry.

The one hundred and sixty three sheep of assorted ages were Hampshires, the four swine were Berkshires, and the three ducks were probably just happy, because ducks are like that.

Amongst the implements of torture, the mere mention of which brings back cruel memories, could be found a grindstone, cross-cut saws, hay-knife and scythes. The list of torturing instruments in the Wash house and Laundry hardly bears contemplation. Amongst the desks and slates, which, it seems, had been bought with money subscribed by the islanders, in the school, there was also a 'Grandmother's chair'.

The length of service of those who thus subscribed, and worked with the farm implements, speaks well for the employers. The same names and families predominated throughout the century and it is not perhaps without interest to look more closely at some of them. We can think our own thoughts as to what the stories of some of them could have been, with their hopes and their disappointments, their joys and their sorrows.

Take John Banner, for example. I wonder who John Banner was. There was no mention of him anywhere else until the 1881 *Census Returns* at the age of forty-five. He was a general labourer and had come from Carew. Living with him were his daughter Mary Ann, two boys Henry and Phillip, also working as general labourers, and the youngest girl, Sarah, in school. Mary Ann was the housekeeper, so maybe John Banner was a widower. In February, 1887, Sarah died on Caldey at the age of eighteen, and three years later Mary Ann died. She was thirty-four and had not married, so perhaps she had sacrificed and stayed single to care for the family. Such things have been known to happen. John Banner died on Caldey in 1899 at the age of sixty-four. A sad story, perhaps, was the story of John Banner. I said perhaps, because, when he died, his death was recorded by his widow Ann Mitchell Banner, who made her mark. And, ten years earlier, in 1889, we find the entry for the birth of Elfrida Banner, the daughter of John Banner, boatman, and his wife Ann Mitchell Banner, late Banner and formerly Goodridge. Maybe in those later years he married his brother's widow. So maybe, too, with bright, childish laughter about the house, to ease the sorrow of the two he had lost, his story was not altogether sad, and I don't suppose we shall ever know.

Up at the lighthouse, earlier in the century, there had been a full family life. Thomas Eadington was the lighthouse keeper, and he and his wife, Isobella, had come from Northumberland. They had ten children, all born on Caldey, between 1835 and 1855. Two of them died when they were young and that was sad for the family, but there was also the happier side. Three of their daughters married whilst they were on the island. The eldest, Margaret Elizabeth, in 1856 married one of the Thomas clan, another James, and a brother to William (Alan, the present Caldey boatman's grandfather). That particular James Thomas also called his son James, just to keep the name in the family, and the son carved out his own niche in Tenby, where he was a plumber and known as 'Spatch', by living to be over a hundred and walking up to Heywood Lane faithfully for every home game to watch his beloved Tenby United play rugby until not long before he died in 1973.

All the lighthouse families were not as permanent as the Eadingtons. William Lightfoot was a Londoner and his wife, Mary, was from the Scilly Islands. I suppose they met there, romance again, and their two children were born at St Ann's Head. Presumably they were at the lighthouse there before coming to Caldey where they were living in 1871.

Also on the island in 1871 was Sarah Franks, who had come from Laugharne to work with the Hawksleys as a nursemaid before Ann Davies had arrived to serve in that capacity. Sarah was thirty and a widow, which sounds like a sad story. But in 1876, on October 27th, (and I had to notice that, because it is my birthday), she married Thomas Morgan who had gone to Caldey from Crunwere to work on the farm. They had two daughters and were still on the island when Tom died in 1904. Henry James (Engineman) went across to register the particulars having been present at the death.

So Thomas Morgan was there in 1881. But it is not only the Thomas family and the James family and the Rowes and the Webbs who can cause confusion. For, in 1881, there was also another Thomas Morgan there, but he had come from Amroth, which is the next parish to Crunwere. His wife, Mary, had come from Ciffig. Their first two children had been born at Ludchurch, where there were limestone quarries, but George, who was a scholar and eleven years of age, had been born on the island, so they had been there for some time. Living with them was Elizabeth Sutcliffe, aged twenty-one, and her baby daughter, Matilda. Elizabeth was their daughter, a dressmaker, who had married a mason, William Sutcliffe, from Tenby. So, had she 'gone home to her mother', (I don't think they did as much of it in those days), or was she just visiting, or gone over to help with some sewing for the family? Tom was still there with Mary in 1881 and George was with them, like his father, working on the farm. Mary died there five years later, and we shall have to wait for the 1891 *Census Returns* to become available before we can have a better idea as to what happened after that.

Perhaps at this stage I feel like Paul must have felt when he wrote to the Hebrews 'And what shall I more say? For the time would fail me to tell of . . . .'. Yes, there are so many of them. But I think I ought to say something of my own grandparents, although they were not there very long. Gramfer probably told somebody to go and get knotted, or take a jump in the sea, or whatever it was they used to say in the old days. I think he must have been a bit like that, because some years after he left Caldey he was farming down at Maiden Wells, near Pembroke, at a little place called Clover Hill, where he was a tenant of Col. Saurin of Orielton. I was thinking about this because, when I was researching for this book, I was glancing through Murray Mathew's book and he gave the figures of the birds taken by Col. Saurin in the duck decoys on Orielton ponds between 1877 and 1888. And it was through Col. Saurin's gamekeeper that the trouble started.

Apparently Gramfer and the gamekeeper were in the pub, and both of them had had a few too many, and one word followed another, as will often happen when two characters have had a few too many, and the gamekeeper said that he had a couple of sows at home that were better looking than Gramfer's daughters. And I can understand Gramfer getting upset because, apart from any other considerations, the girls were good looking. My mother was a beauty, and I have a picture to prove it. So the upshot of it all was that Gramfer told the gamekeeper that he wouldn't let him shoot at Clover Hill again, and the gamekeeper told Col. Saurin what Gramfer had said. There was an old-fashioned notion amongst landlords at that time that they could do what they liked with their own, so Col. Saurin called on Gramfer to see what it was all about, and Gramfer told him he was not going to vote for the

Tories either, because he was a Liberal, And, by all account, for Gramfer to have told Col. Saurin that had the same effect as if he had threatened to sprinkle the Devil with Holy Water, and Gramfer had to go.

Before that, however, he had been for a number of years as a gardener at Cresselly, and all the children were born there, apart from the first one, who was born on Caldey. Gramfer, whose name was John Jones, was a great gardener and came from Abercych, near Boncath. How he met my grandmother, Martha Herbert, who was working on Skomer at the time, I do not know, but they married at Walwyns Castle parish church in 1875, made their first home on Caldey when 'Ned of Caldey' was still there, and my mother's sister was born there in 1876. My grandmother died before I was born, and I was only a small boy when Gramfer died. My mother died in childbirth when I was born, so I know little about it at first hand, but my aunt always told me that there were two babies to be christened in the little church on the island that day, and the other was a boy, and both young couples, each with their first-born, were anxious to have the honour of having their baby done first, because it was to be the first baby to be christened there for goodness knows how long, and the first since something special had been done with the church, whatever it was, but my aunt was not sure about that. So the young curate who had gone over to the island to christen them, being something of a diplomat, solved the problem by saying 'Ladies first'. So my mother's sister was christened first although the other baby, the boy, was older.

I must confess to being a little uneasy about her reference to its being the first christening in the church for such a long time. The two previous entries for Caldey births in the Tenby register have the word 'Private' in the margin. The last one before those two was for Muriel Emily Hawksley, in February of the same year.

My aunt was quite right about the other details, however, for the boy had been born in February and my mother's sister, Margaret Eleanor, in June. They were christened on August 27th. The boy, John William, was the son of Alfred and Elizabeth Rees, but maybe I had better not start on yet another family tree.

When Gramfer left Clover Hill he went to Whitlow farm, at
Saundersfoot (the farm has all been built on now), and there he
remained until the end of his days as a farmer and market
gardener. My grandmother had a shop in the village where she
sold the produce. It is the shop which the present Caldey monks
now run during the summer, which is perhaps as it should be in a
book which seeks to tell the Caldey story. And I have a faded
picture to prove that as well.

Chapter 14

Ambitious plans

The main aspects of the story of Caldey in the present century have already been fully chronicled, particularly in respect of the monastic life and developments. Peter Anson, in his book *Abbot Extraordinary*, gave a detailed account of how the Rev. Done Bushell was instrumental in bringing the Benedictines to Caldey, and how the present monastery came to be built. As far as I was competent to do so I dealt with the coming of the present Cistercian Community, and their life there since, in *Total Community*. There is little to be added on that subject.

Peter Anson was much criticised in some quarters when his book was published, and the criticism continues, especially for his disclosures and assessment of Aelred Carlyle who built the monastery. Peter Anson had failed to come to terms with monasticism

Peter Anson

Rev. W. Done Bushell and Mrs. Mary Done Bushell

himself, and his somewhat erratic and rather less than gracious behaviour in his last years tended to lend support to those critics who say he was himself unstable anyway. Even so, his opinions apart, the book is a remarkable and painstaking record of many historical facts. And, in fairness to him, there was still much which he left unsaid.

The life of Done Bushell was comprehensively covered in a book, *William Done Bushell of Harrow*, published in 1919. He was a fine scholar and an all round athlete. As a schoolmaster, epitomising his own wide interests, he believed that a boy should know something of everything and everything of something. Above all, however, he was a good man, and a man of God.

For the greater part, his life was devoted to Harrow, where he was a Senior Mathematics master, housemaster and, eventually, chaplain at the famous public school. The father of ten children, he bought Caldey in 1897, mainly for the benefit of a mentally retarded son, to shelter him from the gaze of an unsympathetic world. Bushell was nearly sixty years of age at the time, but he threw himself into the work of restoration with great enthusiasm, actually bringing the Priory chapel back into a fit state for worship after centuries of neglect.

As an Anglican priest he was very Catholic in his thinking. A fellow clergyman, the Rev. E. C. E. Owen, wrote of him, 'He used a beautiful prayer in daily service in Caldey Chapel in which he commended the souls of the monks who used to worship there to the mercy of God. That always seemed to me real catholicity, reaching to the heart of things.' And when the Anglican Benedictines of Caldey embraced the Roman Catholic faith in 1913 he continued to befriend them. Again, as Owen wrote of him, 'Tolerance with him was a positive quality. He did not simply refuse to blame those who differed from him; he fastened on what he thought admirable in them, and praised it enthusiastically.'

As far as Caldey was concerned, Bushell used it as a holiday home.

I have found nothing to indicate whether he worked the quarry. Bearing in mind the earlier reference to royalties from the quarry I would suspect that he did not. There are the references in various agreements to cottages let to quarrymen, farm hands and gardeners, to suggest that somebody was working the quarry. It may or may not have been Bushell, but by this time the trade had fallen away.

We know for certain that, after an unsatisfactory attempt to farm the island, with the aid of a quick succession of Scottish bailiffs, he let the farm, in 1902, to a tenant, for £200 a year. The tenant was John Roblin Thomas, a Pembrokeshire man, who had been farming near Clarbeston Road. The landlord retained the gardens and greenhouses and certain rights, including the rabbits, and the exclusive use of Drinkim Bay for himself and family. Part of the agreement arranged for Thomas to supply '30 loads of farmyard manure at 3/6 per load to the gardens annually.'

Subsequently Thomas asked for a lease and this was granted, in 1904, for fourteen years, with a clause that he would receive £2,000 should he be disturbed during that time. Bushell had paid Cuninghame £3,782-13s.-6d. ingoing when he bought the island, but there is no record of how much he received from his tenant by way of ingoing.

The cottages, except the farmhouse where Thomas lived, were also retained by Done Bushell and 'let to quarrymen, farm hands and gardeners at 1/- per week.' The original agreement also specified other conditions and privileges to which Thomas was a party, such as:

> . . . and will supply the lessor and his tenants and agents with horses and carts for the Conveyance of corn produce luggage and all other effects things from and to the landing stage at two shillings and sixpence for each load whenever required and will at all times pursuant to ancient custom allow Henry James Engineman and his successors in that employment without compensation to the lessee for loss of time to assist in loading the vessels with stone or other materials.
>
> Loading—Farm hands will be allowed by Mr Thomas to assist in the loading of the vessels according to the custom of the Island as heretofore being paid for their time by the Captains of the Vessels.
>
> Government Contracts—Mr Thomas will take over the existing arrangements with Lighthouse and Post Office (which are much to his

An early view of the village—the James family outside their house

Lizzie James (left) with the rest of the island children, c.1903

advantage). There is a quarterly payment of 5/- for a cart and 5/- also for every cart required at any other time, and 3/6 a day for a man's work for any purpose. The P.O. pays Mr Thomas £5 a year as Post Master (we cart up all the Lighthouse Stores).

Subsequently Thomas asked for the use of two cottages for his workmen and this was agreed to.

In June 1899, eighteen months after buying the island, Done Bushel had raised a mortgage of £6,000, presumably to finance the programme of renovations on which he had embarked. Although the family used Caldey mainly as a holiday home, they took a keen interest in the island and its people. A letter which Mrs Bushell wrote to engineman Henry James' ten year old daughter Lizzie, in February, 1903, typifies the relationship and attitude:

> My dear Lizzie, I am much pleased with your neatly written, well-spelt letter. I feel sure you must be profitting by Miss Woodruffe's teaching. I shall hope to see the new sums you have been learning when I am next on Caldey. I very nearly came with the Master. I am much looking forward to seeing the beautiful birds which will now be beginning to visit our pretty Island once more. Please remember me to all my Island's friends and believe me to be
> Yours very faithfully
> Mary Bushell.

In 1906 Done Bushell sold the island to Benjamin Fearnley (Dom Aelred) Carlyle and his Anglican Benedictine monks for £12,000, which was £200 less than the price for which he had bought it, so that, bearing in mind all the restoration work which had been done, he added his name to the long list of those who had spent and lost large sums of money there. He did, however, retain the use of the Priory mansion for himself and his family, and continued to have an interest in the island until his death, at the age of seventy-nine, in 1917. He had also left £8,000 of the purchase price as a private mortgage for five years.

Carlyle and his followers had spent a brief time on the island five years previously, but now they came back as owners. The whole story has already been told in sufficient detail to warrant little repetition here, but it meant that for the next decade there was the joint influence of Aelred Carlyle and Done Bushell on the island people and all that was happening.

I heard much of this era, when I was younger, from one of life's characters, Arthur Gay, who worked with us as a gardener years ago at Amroth. He had worked, as a young man, in the gardens at Caldey, and I heard many a story about the island from him.

He was a first-class gardener and used to love to tell how he was with Ernie Bulpitt, the head-gardener on Caldey, when he developed in the greenhouses there the cucumber which he named *Edney's Market Champion* after his wife. Bulpitt's wife, Edith, gave birth to their daughter, Mary Teresa, on Caldey in 1909. *Edney's Market Champion* reached the market as a Novelty in 1913 in the catalogue of 'Watkins and Simpson', the Leicester seed firm, and a development from it, the *Telegraph (Edney's)* remained in their catalogue until 1968.

Carlyle, having bought the island, immediately embarked on a vast programme of capital expenditure, which was to continue until the financial chickens came home to roost a decade or so

Before the early 20th century building began

later. More restoration work was done on the old Priory church
and so, for a brief period at the beginning of the century, Anglican
services were held there. These had already been started for the
villagers by Done Bushell, and now the monks were able to
worship there as well. At the same time more restoration work
was being done on the much older village church of St. David's.

Some of the old cottages were pulled down and new houses
built, with a complete sewerage system and piped water supply
for the whole island. A Guest House, subsequently to become
known as St Philomena's, was built near, and of stones from, one
of the old quarries. A row of workmen's cottages was built on top
of the cliff above the village. Eventually these were occupied as a
temporary monastery, until the monastery, as we now know it,
was built a few years later. A shop and club room were built, and
the island post office, which had previously been up at the well-
house in the farmyard, was established there. A village hall was
built, and Carlyle, who had a great sense of the theatrical, had it

Looking across 'The Barracks' and The Common. The old road from the jetty is
to the left of St. Philomena's

The Common in the 1920s and in 1953

expensively equipped for stage productions. The old 'Barracks' was converted into a power-house where an electric generator was installed, and a new wooden building, later to be known as St Joseph's, was built on the edge of the Common to house some of the army of workers. The house known as Tŷ Gwyn was built to accommodate the Island Steward, Mr Pomeroy, and a flight of steps built leading up from the Common. The Common was what developed after the original Priory Bay became silted up. The house now known as Tŷ Mair was built for Carlyle's mother, Anna Maria, and named Casa Maria after her.

The electric generator was 'a dynamo driven by a powerful suction gas engine.' When the village hall opened in 1911 there were two hundred people at the supper. In the course of all this work trenches were discovered above the old lime-kiln to the east of Priory Bay, but no one has ever established when they were dug, or for what purpose.

The quarry at High Cliff was again brought into production by Carlyle, with the installation of much expensive equipment and a new jetty. William Alun Jones, who had been the quarry manager

High Cliff quarry, c.1913

William Alun Jones, quarry manager in the 1890s, came back to Tenby in 1912 to reopen the quarries for Aelred Carlyle and advise on machinery

in the 1890s, came to advise him. This project, too, like so many of his other ventures, was doomed. The development of the internal combustion engine was about to make road transport much cheaper.

The cottage monastery, as it became known, and the new church, were built from stone from the quarry at the foot of the cliffs on which the monastery stands. The monastery itself was built between the years of 1910 and 1913, and, when the High

CALDEY. THE VILLAGE.

1908   After the building of the workmen's cottages which became the temporary monastery

Cliff quarry was re-started, stone was brought from there for the purpose. This was done by means of a crane above High Cliff. I have been told that a railway ran from the crane to the monastery. There is no record of it, and I have not heard of any remains of such a railway coming to light, apart from an old road from the top of High Cliff.

Carting stones from the quarry beneath the monastery

1923   The monastery and church have been built, and a number of old cottages demolished

The cottages and an interesting view in the 1920s

The island ketch, *Cornish Lass*, which was active in this trade whilst it lasted, was skippered by Jack Childs, a redoubtable sea-faring character from my native Saundersfoot, where he was known as 'Geethy', and who could easily warrant a chapter on his own. The war, however, marked the virtual end of this venture.

It has not been easy to fix the date when the quarries closed, but the September issue of *Pax* in 1922 carries an interesting reference which says:

'It is rumoured that Caldey quarries are to be re-opened.' So says a local newspaper that lies before us; and for once Dame Rumour is not a lying jade. She is only slightly inaccurate; she has put the future tense in place of the present. The fact is that the island quarries have now been busily at work for some little time past. As our readers probably know, it was the great war that brought operations to a temporary standstill. The men were called up; the boats were commandeered; and building work everywhere was suspended. We naturally hoped the close of war would quickly be followed by a restoration of normal conditions; but, as everybody knows, this was not the case, and it is not till now that we have the pleasure of seeing

The workmen on Caldey, c.1913

Tenby workmen crossing to Caldey in the *Firefly*, c.1912

Don Aelred with the workmen building the monastery

the quarrymen once more at work and the long-idle machinery again in motion.

The article then went on to laud the past glories and the quality product of the Caldey quarries. This was perfectly true, for time was when they had also produced a fine specimen of black 'marble'. But the optimistic note was typical of the many references in *Pax* during those years, when the various commercial ventures were embarked on and, as often as not, as quickly abandoned.

Hard facts on the quarrying business are scarce, but Ivor John of Tenby reckons that work there ceased in 1921. He acknowledges that memory plays funny tricks and that it could have been 1922. But, at the age of fifteen, he helped to load the last two boats. Twenty years later he was to be one of the members of the Tenby fire brigade who volunteered to go over to fight the huge war-time fire which destroyed the cottage monastery and damaged the chapel and so much besides.

Ivor was another stalwart of the marvellous pre-war Tenby rugby team. He was working with my father at the time, building St Bride's Hotel in Saundersfoot, and I can remember my father paying the men at Saturday mid-day and saying, 'Now then, Ivor John first, for he's got to jump on the bike for Tenby to play.' What he would have been earning with my father in 1932 I don't know, but he said that, ten years earlier, when he was working on Caldey building Tŷ Chwarel, the money for labourers tending the masons was 3/4 a day. Work was also going on at the monastery, and eight volunteers were needed to load the two boats. Ivor was one of the volunteers and the work was very heavy, because the loading had to be done in four hours, which was two hours each side of high tide. For loading the boat of a hundred tons the eight men received 4d a ton, or ½d each per ton. So that worked out at 4/2 each for four hours, as against 3/4 for a day tending the masons. But they reckoned they earned it, and I would not be the one to dispute their belief.

That is the nearest I have been able to come to establishing the date when quarrying came to an end on Caldey. In the archives there is a copy of a lease, dated Sept. 6th, 1922, on the limestone quarries and the sand and gravel pits, between the Benedictines and The Roadstone Company Ltd. Who or what they were I have no idea, nor have I found any record of their ever having worked there.

Ben Waters, of Kilgetty, who, in conjunction with W. G. Thomas of Coedcanlas, was active in road haulage at that time, had some stones from Caldey for road surfacing, but there is no record of The Roadstone Company or whether Ben Waters had any connection with it.

Chapter 15

Days of change

Done Bushell was one of the early members of the Society for Psychical Research. Aelred Carlyle had a lifelong interest in the mystic and would tell ghost stories for hours on end. During those early years on Caldey he visited Glastonbury at a time when archaeological work and certain psychical experiments were being carried out there. Small wonder that the origin of the story often told on Caldey, of the Glastonbury treasure and the Black Monk, can be dated to this time. Carlyle maintained that he had many times seen a black-habited monk in the lane near the old Priory. Other people had also seen this apparition which, or who, had vanished as suddenly as it, or he, had appeared.

Miss Renée Haynes, of the Society for Psychical Research, who has some considerable knowledge of the subject, visited Caldey a few times between 1920 and 1923 and stayed in the island Steward's house, Tŷ Gwyn. The ghost and spirit talk was still very much in evidence. As she pointed out, the stories of bumps and movement of stones up at the old Priory in the dead of night could well have been related to underground caverns which run back from the Cathedral Caves. The boomings from underground water when there is a heavy swell can be considerable.

There was also the story of the White Lady seen not far from Tŷ Gwyn and, as Miss Haynes said, 'My mother used to think that she was that lady. She slept badly and would sometimes come out in her dressing gown to look at the stars or the sea, and to breathe in the peace of the night.'

Stories were also told about hearing Paul Jones and his pirates burying treasure. 'This, oddly enough,' said Miss Haynes, 'happened to me one evening, when dusk was darkening. I'd gone on to the terrace to enjoy the last embers of sunset, the lights beginning to twinkle in Tenby on the mainland, and the silence, almost unimaginable today—no wireless, no telly, no night-flying planes, only the mild splash of the ebb tide below, and gentle voices chatting in the house. The monastery was dark, there were no lights in the village, and no one could have seen to dig. Then I heard quite clearly the sound of iron spades digging down through sand and pebbles and occasionally striking rock. I was puzzled as to what it could be, but did not at first think of the legend—and when it came to my mind, oddly enough I wasn't scared.'

There were other stories and much psychic talk, particularly about the Black Monk. Whether or not there is anything in all this sort of thing is not for me to say. There are experiences which cannot be explained. But I firmly believe that if you dwell on this subject long enough you can get your mind in such a twist that you will believe anything. If you are expecting to see something, sooner or later you will see it, or something like it. Arthur Gay assured me that he was going round the greenhouse boilers late one night when he saw a monk in a black habit walking towards him. Gay pulled his forelock and said 'Goodnight Brother.' But Brother disappeared through a door in the wall where no door was, but where, so they said, a doorway had once been. It would be difficult to imagine a more hard-bitten character than Gay, and it shows the dangers of listening too much to the sort of talk which was no doubt rife on Caldey at that time.

Hard-bitten? Let one story serve to illustrate the point. One of the brothers was going overseas on a pilgrimage and taking with him a statue of the Blessed Virgin and Child. Gay and another workman were in the church crating up the statue, and Dom Aelred was there supervising and hovering about generally. Gay was an excitable, dashing sort of character who took his work seriously and conscientiously. His colleague, in passing, brushed against the statue, which began to wobble dangerously, whereupon Gay jumped to grab it and shouted, 'For Christ's sake, Jimmy, watch the bloody image!' And the Abbot, very quietly, said, 'Arthur, our Holy Mother if you please.'

Before dealing in more detail with the influence on island life, however, it could be as well to consider what was happening on the farm.

Mention has already been made of the clause in John Roblin

Thomas's lease to the effect that he would receive £2,000 compensation in the event of his being disturbed before the expiration of the lease. I had the benefit of several long talks with Mr Stuart Thomas, when in his eighties, the son of John Thomas, and there are also some interesting and enlightening papers in the collection of the Carmarthen Records Office. From these it is clear that Carlyle was a difficult man with little idea of business. The question of settling for the few things he was taking over from Done Bushell dragged on interminably, and eventually had to be settled by arbitration. The copy of Thomas's lease of 1904 had been so heavily underlined in pencil in certain places, and in the margin, that it had evidently been the subject of much scrutiny on some subsequent occasion.

In 1909 there was correspondence from Br Illtud, on behalf of Fr Abbot, enquiring about the legal position concerning the rabbits which, it was claimed, were increasing so rapidly that they would have to be regarded as vermin. The correspondence did not say so, but doubtless they were doing considerable damage in the gardens. So would this be the grounds of some sort of case against the farmer? And the answer, of course, was that under the terms of the lease the landlord had retained the rabbits, so Carlyle had already bought and paid for them, which meant that he had no level on this score to take any action against the tenant. 'We note,' wrote Br Illtud, 'that they were paid for and conclude that we cannot do anything in the matter.'

What, then, was it all about?

John Thomas, farming on the mainland, had five children and, needing a bigger place, had decided, with his wife, to go to Canada. They were in the process of negotiating when it was realised there was a sixth baby on the way, so all thoughts of Canada, for the time being at any rate, had to be abandoned. At the same time Done Bushell advertised for a tenant for his farm on Caldey, and the same pioneering spirit which would have taken John Thomas to Canada now took him to the island. Stuart was the sixth child, and he was eight weeks old when he went to Caldey with his parents and their young family in the spring of 1902. He was a growing lad by the time the new landlords came

John R. Thomas, the last farm tenant of Caldey

Stuart Thomas, son of the last farm tenant on Caldey

and he remembered clearly how the situation developed, for Carlyle embarked on a campaign of harassment.

'The Abbot,' Stuart Thomas said, 'would take the monks walking through the corn fields and leave all the gates open. In the end father waited for him coming through the farmyard and they fought. So there was only one outcome to that. Father gave him a hiding. He was bred right for it. Irish on one side and Welsh on the other. Then he put up notices "Trespassers Will Be Prosecuted" and after that there was no more trouble.'

Eventually Carlyle realised that the compensation clause in the lease would have to be honoured if he wanted possession of the farm, and John Thomas left the island, in the autumn of 1911 to farm at Alleston near Pembroke. He was a hard-working man and did well on Caldey, especially with the compensation.

During his time on the island he kept the traditional Shorthorns, sheep, pigs and corn and, as would be expected, Stuart was able, like all the islanders, to tell interesting stories of his boyhood days.

One early memory was of a time when he was a boy, and his father went down the cliff, by means of a rope fastened to a bar, to a ewe that was stranded. The ewe went back up by another way, the rope came off the bar, and then it was John Thomas who was stranded. He was rescued eventually when he was spotted from a boat by some of the monks who were out fishing. They brought him back and then he sent young Stuart to fetch his jacket, which he had taken off and left on the ground before going down the cliff. Stuart found the jacket all right, but the dog was guarding it and, good pals though they were, he refused to let Stuart touch it. Stuart went home and told his father, only to be sent back again. But again it was in vain and eventually John Thomas had to fetch the jacket himself.

These cliff descents have always caused trouble for island farmers, as the sheep nibble further and further down in search of the green and tasty morsels and eventually find themselves unable to return. There are also the cases of wild panic of sheep unused to such conditions, as was the case when John Thomas went away to a sheep sale to Gloucester and wired home that he had bought five Suffolk rams, which he had put on the train, and saying to put them in a certain field. The rams arrived safely and were turned out according to instructions. They were never seen again, the cliffs having claimed them all.

Another particularly interesting recollection was of an occasion when they were taking a load of porkers over to Tenby on the *Firefly*. The tide was out, however, and as it was therefore not possible to land in the harbour, the pigs were tipped out into the sea off St Catherine's and they swam ashore onto the beach. I find this particularly interesting because, although I have never witnessed it happening, I had always been told, and believed, that pigs could not swim because their front feet coming up would cut their throats. Stuart Thomas said he had always heard the same story, but that certainly those pigs that day had reached the shore without mishap.

Perhaps Stuart's most significant recollection, however, in so far as it points to the island customs, is of the cattle which were slaughtered on the island. Yet another star of the pre-war Tenby rugby side, butcher Wynford Mabe, remembered well as a boy going over with his father to slaughter there, and Wynford's grandfather used to go before that.

We have already seen what George Owen had to say about the purveyors for the pirates making their commissions there, and we have seen how Fanny Price Gwynne commented upon the provisioning of vessels which obviated the necessity of costly transport by boat to the mainland. At other times Caldey has usually had the use of a fair sized boat. All in all, and this is something I have long suspected, there may not have been as much swimming of cattle to the mainland as has so often been supposed. True, it has been done from time to time, but probably not on a great scale.

At one time the present community of Cistercians were having to swim cattle across to the South Beach and were landing them near Giltar. The legendary Brother Thomas was in charge and one wretched bullock, after the perverse manner of its kind, took off up into the town, with Brother, sandals and habit flapping, in hot pursuit. The chase came to an end in the rectory gardens, where the bullock pranced across the lawn and set about the flowers and cabbages. Far from showing any anxiety to drive the marauder out, Brother actually slammed the gate shut with a whoop of triumph to have thus confined the fugitive what time he could wait for assistance to arrive. It was at this juncture that the rector emerged from the house, waving his arms in considerable agitation, and shouting not very polite words. But Brother shouted back, 'It's all right, rector! Don't worry—it's not a papal bull.'

For the record, it is of interest that Stuart Thomas, after arrival on the island in 1902, was baptised in the village church of St David's. Done Bushell was at that time restoring the Priory church and, in 1906, Stuart's sister was baptised there, but there is no entry in the Tenby or Penally church registers of either service.

In the 1917 autumn edition of *Pax* there is another significant item because the lease on the Priory had terminated with the death of Done Bushell that year. The writer said that since 1913 there were Anglicans, about twelve altogether, still living on the island and 'working for us,' who were still using the Priory church, 'and now that it is to be restored to Catholic worship, suitable provision will, of course, be made for their needs.' The population consisted of eighty-four Catholics and twenty non-Catholics. The numbers did not include people at the light house and coast guard stations—'for whom we are not responsible.'

These figures, although they probably included the monks, are significant, for they show what had happened in the space of the four years since the Benedictines had embraced the Roman Catholic faith. The Catholicism on Caldey at that time had all the enthusiasm of the convert, unfortunately so often unthinking and unyielding. Forty years later that marvellous scholar and thinker, Ronald Knox, himself a convert, observed, in an article in *Pax* in the spring of 1956, how the religion of the Caldey of those earlier years had all the trappings of Catholicism without any allegiance to, or understanding of, the dogma. Before the conversion, when it had bordered on Catholicism, it had perhaps been even worse and more bewildering for the old-fashioned, insular villagers, who must have wondered what had hit them.

A news item in the 1913 Michaelmas edition of *Pax* said, 'As we have now four priests in residence at Caldey, there are several Masses each day, one being said in the old parish church of St David. The oratory of Our Lady Star of the Sea, formed in the old watch-tower on the cliff, has also been in constant use by priests staying at the Guest-house.'

In those early days Br John Blaker acted as the parish priest.

It was an atmosphere of all action, all stations go, with the typical song and dance of the convert. On the face of it there was also a lively social side, with splendid theatrical productions on the splendidly equipped stage of the newly built village hall. Programmes remain to tell of the performers. Ralph Pomeroy was the steward, for whom Tŷ Gwyn had been built in 1911. But who was Miss F. Banner? Was she young Elfrida on whose family we speculated earlier? We know who Lizzie James was. She was the daughter of Henry James, Engineman, whose forebears had been

Br John Balker who acted as parish priest, 1912

on Caldey since time out of mind. She had been written to, as a small girl, in terms of encouragement by Mrs Bushell. But things were not quite the same now. It was suddenly realised that parties were being held to which only the Catholic children were being invited, and the others were left to feel out in the cold. So Lizzie, like some of the others, drifted away from the island. Be it remembered also that it was a time of vast financial insecurity in the island's affairs. It was a time of great change.

On the other hand, there were those who were devoted to Abbot Carlyle, who had so much personal charm.

In 1914, for example, old John Webb died in the ancient cupboard bed which had slept untold generations of Webbs before him. A newspaper report of the time said:

> Recently there passed to his rest a figure familiar to all who have known Caldey—old John Webb. He was in his seventy-fifth year; and in him, as Mr Bushell said at the funeral, we have lost one who represented in a special degree the old life of Caldey. For John had been born, lived and died on the island, in the same cottage just below the Monastery, where the Webbs have lived for generations. He had many stories to tell concerning local history and topography, and he could give a vivid picture of the invasion of Pembrokeshire by the French in 1797, when his grandfather lived on the island. For many weeks he had been laid low with heart trouble, but kept himself alive, as the doctor and those round him declared, by sheer force of his desire to live until Father Abbot came home again. His wish was fulfilled, and he sank peacefully on the second day after the Abbot's return. He was buried on the Thursday by Mr Bushell in the little village churchyard.

In June, Dom Aelred had written to John Webb from Maredsous. He wrote:

> I am so very sorry to hear from Brother Wilfred that you are in such a poorly condition of health, but I know he is doing all that is possible for you, and he tells me that Doctor Drake is attending you.
>
> Only a few weeks now and I shall be with you again at Caldey: so you must take every care to keep well and strong that you may be among those at the slip to welcome me home. Hearts are troublesome things when they get out of order, and yours is evidently giving you a

John Webb and his wife, Eliza

good deal of pain; so you must keep very fit and do just as you are told.

Give my love to Eliza and tell her to keep cheerful and not spend her time moaning and wringing her hands over you. I want to see two smiling old Webbs when I get back to Caldey on July 31st.

Believe me, my dear John,

Your affectionate

Fr Aelred O.S.B.

Carlyle had been to Belgium where, in a matter of months, he had made his solemn profession and been ordained as a priest. Although the Catholic Church is so often spoken of as being unyielding, it had unbent to the extent of allowing him to do, in eight months, something which would normally have taken a monk seven or eight years. He returned on July 31st and John Webb died on August 2nd. John's wife, Eliza, died at Monkton near Pembroke, the following June, where she had gone to live with her married daughter.

Whilst the old island families were moving out, new families were moving in. And, of course, the relationship was usually a good one. It is perhaps typified by a report in the summer edition of *Pax* in 1915 on the occasion of the celebration of Corpus Christi.

> With us it is essentially a family festival, a summer Christmas; and both Monastery and Village share in the work of preparation and in the actual joys and devotions of the day. To a discerning eye there is a

Whatever the nature of the event, it was raining. Early 1920s. The old boathouse, formerly a lime-kiln and now an electricity sub-station is in the left-hand corner beyond 'The Barracks'

sense of unusual quiet in the Village during the early morning, and one might know that something is going to happen. Presently a Brother, intent upon a dozen things which must be done before the afternoon, is stopped by an Islander who, with serious concern upon his brow, tells him, 'The flags from Chapel Point have not come down yet. Last year they were brought in the donkey cart, but Jessie is down at the slip this morning, Brother, and what can we do?' The difficulty must be considered gravely without sign that the precious moments are passing all too quickly; a compromise is effected: the flags are carried down by hand as far as the Priory gate (they are a heavy load), and it is arranged that others shall bring them into the village. There are further difficulties to solve: Islanders seek the advice of willing Bretheren, the monks bespeak the help of kindly villagers. There are few hidden preparations or 'surprises'. Every one knows what his neighbour is going to put out on their window sills, what flags that family will hang.

To that extent Caldey has not changed much in the intervening years.

What was lost, of course, with a complete upheaval of the island population, was a wealth of legend and marvellous stories which would have been handed down from one generation to another. This, perhaps more than any other reason, is why so little of the island lore remains. Those who would have had stories handed down to them have been scattered, literally, to the four corners of the earth.

Chapter 16

More island people

Following the departure of John Thomas as tenant in 1911, the farm reverted to the monks. Dom Aelred switched all his monks from one job to another with bewildering rapidity, so it was small wonder that there was a similar coming and going of staff, many of whom have long since been forgotten.

In his Community letter in June 1910 the Abbot had mentioned that W. L. Moss had taken the Oblate Brother's place as Island Steward. The Oblate Brother was Br Illtud who had been writing about the rabbits and acting as Island Steward unpaid. Before throwing in his lot for a time with the Benedictines he was, in private life, Bryan Burstall, and it was he who found the money to make purchase of the island possible. In December the Abbot had reported that, when the tenant left next year, W. L. Moss would take over as 'he understands farming and is thoroughly keen about it.' So W. L. Moss would be busy in his dual role.

I have met quite a few people in my time who understand farming and are thoroughly keen about it. The following year Tŷ Gwyn was being built for the new steward. On the farm, W. Marsh was in charge of the poultry and signing himself as Manager. But, in September 1914, we read that, 'We are sorry indeed to lose Mr Longhurst, who is taking up work elsewhere this autumn. For more than seven years, first as manager of the poultry yard and later as farm bailiff he has worked indefatigably . . .' Then, in 1916, there is reference to a farm bailiff, Keilly, being replaced by a 'working bailiff' as an economy.

The replacement was a man by the name of Sam Gwyther. He was a good farmer who had learned his job on that well-known Pembrokeshire farm on the shores of the Cleddau, Coedcanlas. In later years he was to become farm bailiff at Hurst House, Laugharne, which he subsequently bought. The monks would seem to have been pleased with him for, in the summer edition of Pax, a warm tribute was paid to the farm bailiff for the excellent

153

condition of the calves and the fact that two hundred tons of 'top quality hay' had been harvested.

Gwyther, as he was universally known, for his part was not nearly so well pleased. And here again I was fortunate to track down an old gentleman who was a much younger half brother to Gwyther's wife. Gwyther, he said, always reckoned that the Abbot was a 'bloody owld fool' and that the monks were a lot of 'dull buggers'.

Readers from outside Pembrokeshire may well frown, or raise their eyebrows, according to their personal predilection, at the use of such expressions. Pembrokeshire people, however, will know exactly what it means, for it says in those few words what Peter Anson had to take many chapters to try to explain. And Gwyther probably put it better, for no one could read any malice or disloyalty into it. Just bemused, long-suffering, frustrated, good-natured dismay. Gwyther would mow the hay and, with the limited labour at his disposal, work hard to prepare it for harvesting. Then, when it was fit, he would send down to the monastery for the monks to come, as arranged, to help to carry it, only for word to be sent back that they were too busy at prayer or contemplation and to leave it until tomorrow. During the war more land had to be ploughed for the growing of corn. How they managed with that it is difficult to imagine.

Gwyther always said that Pomeroy, the steward, was the only one from whom he could ever get any sense. It was Pomeroy, during John Thomas's time, who built the little bungalow now known as Green Pastures, but nobody has ever been able to make out why it was built. Gwyther was there during the war, along with Pomeroy, but it must have been a difficult time for everybody. And many things were happening.

By the time war broke out work had been going on at the jetty. In December 1914 *Pax* reported, 'The approach to the landing-slip at present suggests a backwoods settlement. Besides the little ramshackle tin shed, which has nevertheless been the most useful of all tin sheds ever erected, and which dates back to the time when Cunningham owned the Island, there is the fisherman's hut where his nets, lobster pots, lines and other tackle are stored; and

The landing slip before 1916

the boathouse with a railroad leading from the crane up to its front doors. There is now a fourth and very necessary building, standing in the corner on the right as you turn from the slip and take to the path. The stores and whatever else is brought over from the mainland will be housed there, and the cart will only need to come down at stated intervals during the week, instead of meeting almost every boat.'

About this time a detachment of coastguards came to Caldey, and one of them was Simon Kidney, who had served in the Royal Navy. He was to stay on as an employee of the Community, mostly as boatman, but also working in the garden and on the farm. He left the island eventually in 1925 and went back to his old job as a coastguard, at Manorbier, where he died three years later. Reporting on this, *Pax* said, 'Many visitors will remember the huge Irish sailor with his fine, weather-beaten face, who ran the old Stella for us, and will probably have many memories of his quiet and dignified courtesy, obliging but unservile—from Cohn.' The *Stella Maris* had been wrecked the year before he left Caldey. I wonder how much influence it had on his decision to leave Caldey. By such happenings are our destinies fashioned.

Repairing the jetty and towing the landing barges into position
(see *Total Community*)

Simon Kidney

The *Stella Maris* was a smart motor launch, which had been purchased originally for the Abbot's personal and private use. Later on she had to be pressed into much more mundane service. When she was wrecked she was bought by Jack Childs, erstwhile skipper of the *Cornish Lass*, to be repaired at Saundersfoot, and I remember her well. But I cannot claim to have sailed in her because my loyalties were with Jack's brother, Jim, with whom I spent countless happy boyhood days, and there was a blood feud between them. It was Jim who, amongst other things, initiated me into the secrets of the sculduggery that goes on in a rugby scrum, which maybe is why I grew up with enough sense to become a threequarter.

Jack Childs, skipper of the *Cornish Lass*

During the first year of the war a wooden retreat was built on the cliffs above Paul Jones' Bay and named The Sambuca after the title of a book, *The Solitaries of the Sambuca*, which had recently been published. In later years it was pulled down and its name lingered on as a puzzle to younger generations as to what was Sambuca and why. At St Joseph's there were boys who had come to Caldey to be trained in gardening, poultry and farm work. When the last attempt was made to revitalise the quarrying, the workers were again housed at St Joseph's, which once more became The Barracks, and they were looked after by Sam Fogwell and his wife, Frances.

It was about this time that one of the monks, Dom Asaph Harris, rather imprudently and absentmindedly, allowed a light to shine out in the black-out from his window. I think he was sleeping in St Martin's tower. The coastguards from Tenby had to draw his attention to it, and it was not long before there were rumours, so typical of war-time, that a German submarine was putting in nightly at Caldey Bay. Echoes of the story were to be heard for a long time.

In the winter of 1915 'Jonah', the Tenby boatman who looked after the monks' stores at Tenby harbour, dropped dead on the harbour. The skipper of the *Firefly* was Joe Davies, usually known as Joe the Hook, because of the hook on his artificial arm. He returned from the island one day about this time to find his wife burned to death. She had been ailing for some months and had apparently been sitting too close to the fire. *Pax* said, 'Skipper Joe is well-known to everyone who comes to Caldey. He has been in charge of the various craft plying between Tenby and the Island for a very long time; and our dear old tub of a *Firefly*, in her twenty-two years' service has scarcely known any other captain.'

It was not long after this tragedy that Joe was to lose his beloved boat also. There was an oft told story on Catholic Caldey that on the *Firefly*'s last voyage to the island, a visitor enquired of the lighthouse keeper, who was a devout Anglican, as to whether she was quite safe. 'Why aye,' he replied. 'She's as safe as the Church of England.' The *Firefly* was wrecked that night. She had been anchored off the New Pier at Tenby until there should be tide in the harbour at 9.30 p.m. A gale blew up, the *Firefly* dragged her anchor, and within twenty minutes was aground at the end of the stone pier. Joe Davies, Tom Davies, the engineer, and Billy Price, the third hand, made valiant efforts to save her, but she was a total loss. As things transpired she was not to be adequately replaced until 1925 when the *Teresina* was purchased. She was named in honour of St Therese, the Little Flower, to whom there had been a special devotion by some of the Community and whom they had asked in their own prayers to intercede for them.

With all their other financial troubles it was a black time for the Community. There was no money to replace the *Firefly* and it was then that the *Stella Maris* was pressed into service. All in all it was just one more example of the truism that troubles never come singly. Not long afterwards Albert Richards, a mason, who had worked faithfully for the Community for many years, fell on his head from a scaffolding in the cloister and his injuries were so serious that he died a few hours afterwards.

The war ended at last and *Pax* commemorated the occasion by referring to the sounding off of guns at Tenby, and the anticipation of any announcement on Caldey by 'Old John Bates' who answered the Tenby guns announcing the armistice with 'a series of gentle explosions, as he stood out and let off some cartridges from his shot-gun. Each report meant so much less for his rabbits and birds: but it was in a good cause.'

I am not sure why he was referred to as 'Old John Bates', except that they say that old age is about fifteen years older than we are ourselves. He lived in the cottage at the foot of the hill and was the official rat-catcher. Gruesome though it may sound it was said of him that he could bite the head off a rat.

On a more auspicious occasion, however, he was designated as a gamekeeper. Abbot Carlyle, in fact, had introduced the breeding of pheasants as one of his many abortive enterprises. The auspicious occasion referred to was the wedding of John Bates, a bachelor of fifty-four years of age and a gamekeeper, to Lily Eden, a spinster of thirty-eight and a cook (she had come to the guest-house as cook) at St Teilo's Roman Catholic Church in Tenby on Nov. 15th, 1919. The ceremony was performed by Dom Ambrose Holly, one of the monks. During that year there had been the business of registering St David's as a 'place of worship for the solemnisation of marriages'. When this had been attended to there were other conditions to be fulfilled before Fr Abbot could become an 'Authorised Person'. *Pax* reported:

> The completion of this business was just too late for the wedding of John Bates with Miss Lily Eden: so they were married in Tenby church in November. It was a very stormy day, and a heavy sea was running before an easterly gale: but the nuptial boat made light of the tempest, and the adventurous wedding party was back again at the landing slip before nightfall. One of the farm waggons had been decorated with flags and little bells, and a couple of arm chairs made into a handsome state coach, which was drawn up to the village, amid much rejoicing and excitement, by the strong arms of the young men. In the following week the first wedding took place in the village church. The bride was Miss Margaret Mary McHardy, daughter of

our farm bailiff: Mr Richard Cummins was the bridegroom, and Fr Abbot as the 'Authorised Person', married them himself.

It was the first Catholic wedding on Caldey for four hundred years, and this was perhaps appropriate in so far as it was the start of a new family connection with the island.

Charles McHardy, who had worked at Fort Augustus Abbey, came down to Caldey from Scotland in the May and started work on June 1st, 1919, succeeding Sam Gwyther as farm bailiff. The records show that he was paid £120 per annum, together with his house rent free, two quarts of milk per day, vegetables from the farm, and corn and meal for his fowls and one pig. As things transpired he was to work on Caldey and remain there almost to the end of his life. In January 1938, however, he was taken ill and taken to Tenby hospital. Later, thanks to the generosity of Mrs Roch, wife of Walter Roch, a wealthy lawyer and former M.P. for Pembrokeshire, who had a house on the island, he was removed to Abergavenny. Too ill to return to Caldey, he was taken by his old friends the Benedictines, who by this time had left Caldey and

Charles McHardy and his family

Charles McHardy (left) and Dick Cummins

removed to Prinknash, and he ended his days there with them, and that was where he was buried.

Charles McHardy and his wife, Mary, had eight children and they were all on Caldey. Margaret, the eldest daughter, worked in the dairy, and it must have been another of these sudden romantic Caldey affairs, for in the November she married Richard Cummins, who was already there, working on the farm, when she arrived.

Richard Cummins, an Irishman from Cork, had served in the Royal Artillery during the war, when he was awarded the Military Medal, and then came to work at Caldey on the farm. Best man at his wedding was his brother, known to generations of visitors to Caldey as 'Uncle Jerry', who remained a bachelor, living on the island to the end of his days in 1973 at the age of seventy-nine. Originally he lived in the Well-house, but later moved into the gardener's cottage up at the farm where he stayed until the end. Although not now in use it is still known as 'Uncle Jerry's'. It was perhaps inevitable that he should become known as Uncle Jerry because a whole generation of Cummins children grew up on Caldey to call him by that name.

Dick Cummins and his family, 1942

Dick Cummins and Margaret moved into the Post Office about 1926. They had seven children and all of them had connections with the island. Dick moved away with his family when he retired in 1952 but they drifted back in turn. Jerry worked the Caldey boat, married on the island, but died tragically at the age of forty-three in 1970. Peter came back to the farm and is now the farm bailiff. His son, Stephen, works alongside him. A grandson of Charles McHardy, Andrew, is steward at the guest house, St Philomena's, with his wife, Sally. Gabriel Cummins runs his boat from Tenby to Caldey in the summer, and works as a carpenter on the island during the winter. So it is that a whole new history of generations of the same family is starting to build up.

In January 1920 a ketch, *Alice*, was on her way to Caldey to serve the island as a cargo boat and to carry stone away from the quarries, but she was wrecked at Breaksea Point, near Penarth, when being brought from Sharpness. The skipper was saved, but two members of the crew were drowned. Small wonder that the quarries ceased working not long afterwards. It was in the following year that Dom Aelred Carlyle left Caldey for Canada. It was in many ways the end of one era and the beginning of another.

'Uncle Jerry' Cummins, 1951

Jerry Cummins (left) and Peter (centre) crossing sheep to Saundersfoot, 1949

Chapter 17

A new Order

At the beginning of 1919 Ralph Pomeroy, who had become a Catholic at the same time as the Benedictine Community, intimated that he wished to resign as Island Steward in order to concentrate on his own business in Cardiff, The Trinidad Asphalt Company, but he continued as a good friend to the monks.

His replacement, whose name has long since been forgotten, was recommended by The Country Gentlemen's Association, but he remained no more than a couple of months. The post was then advertised and, from the short-list of six invited to Caldey for an interview, Captain (military) James Sawbridge was invited to fill the post. He would seem to have been enthusiastic because, when Tŷ Chwarel was built, in 1921, he paid for the work himself with the intention of remaining on the island. Shortly after the departure of Abbot Carlyle for Canada that same year, Captain Sawbridge, for whatever reason, also left Caldey. That was in 1922, and the Community's financial plight was such that he looked to them in vain for financial recompense. After his death the full amount was paid to his widow and his son.

When he left Caldey Sawbridge settled in Saundersfoot, where he set up some sort of commercial station for receiving and transmitting wireless messages. The venture, which was not a success, failed for lack of capital, which is hardly surprising if he was still waiting for the money from the house.

Tŷ Chwarel itself also presented a few problems because it had been built with a flat concrete roof. The chippings came from the quarry. It gave endless trouble and subsequently a span roof had to be superimposed. I thought the fact could just be worth recording for the benefit of generations of archaeologists as yet unborn. That was in 1926, when Miss Edith Alis-Smith was given a lease in return for providing the new roof and carrying out other extensive repairs.

Sawbridge was followed as Island Steward, in 1922, by Commander Cecil Farey (late RN) on the recommendation of his cousin, Monsignor Thomas Newsome, a frequent visitor to Caldey, who had tried to advise Dom Aelred on how best to solve his financial problems. Cmdr Farey stayed until 1926.

Whatever assessments may be made of the Benedictines' failure on Caldey following the departure of their founder it must never be forgotten that their task was completely hopeless. In addition to the massive debts with which they had been saddled, the usual post-war betrayal of the nation's farmers had set in. Even good farmers with strong financial reserves found their way into the bankruptcy courts without having the further hazard and cost of trying to make a success of farming an off-shore island.

They were not without their moments, however, for in 1924 their pedigree Dairy Shorthorn bull, 'Caldey Gildas', won first prize in his class at the Royal Welsh Show, which was held that year at Bridgend. But that expedition would have cost and lost them more money than it could have made.

Dick Cummins with Caldey Gildas, 1st prize at the Royal Welsh Show, 1924

Charles McHardy at work in the hay-field   *G. G. Hoare*

Some charming recollections of these years were recounted by Sr Mary Latham, a Benedictine nun of Fernham, in the 1982 summer edition of *Pax*. She visited Caldey as a girl from the years 1919 to 1926 and wrote, sixty years later:

On arriving at the Slip, as the landing stage is called, Mr Raymond and Pat Mulgrew usually met the passengers to take the luggage and any packages for the monastery and islanders. Mr Raymond had two donkeys and a cart: I cannot remember now whether it was the mother or son that pulled the cart, but I do remember that if the other donkey was heard braying in the distance off would go your luggage until they had had their interview.

Ducks and geese wandered about the island during our early visits. The geese stretched out their long necks and cackled as they approached: this terrified me. The ducks were more friendly, but they came to an end when some sour yeast was thrown out of the monastery kitchen where the bread for the whole island was baked. They ate the yeast and made their way to the pond for a drink. Next morning they were found heads down and legs up.

George Rayment

On the feast of St Samson . . . the evening was spent in dancing,
mostly country dances. Old Mrs Raymond accompanied these
dances on the piano. She would be seen standing at her cottage door
about ten minutes before the time waiting for some passer-by to
fasten all the little press studs at the back of her high-necked blouse.
Invariably you would find on reaching the bottom that one had been
missed, which meant going back to the offender. We had to be careful
not to make much noise on leaving so as not to disturb the monks who
had already retired and would be up early for Matins.

My sister Agnes met her husband in a most amusing way about
1920. We used to go to Compline each evening, and on this occasion a
young man came up outside the church holding a black hair-ribbon,
and glancing at Agnes asked if by any chance it was hers. It wasn't,
but he stayed talking and walking with us. He joined us after
Compline again a few times and then one evening asked my Father if
he might take Agnes by herself. Reg had been briefly in the monastery
and on leaving had joined the group of farm students. It was one of
these who had found the ribbon, and Reg gave him a packet of twenty
cigarettes in return for it.

Mrs. Margaret Cummins with young Richard at the donkey's head and
Peter and Jerry in the cart

Mgr John Mostyn (Canon of St. Peter's Rome)

All this romance again. We use less subterfuge these days.

It is history how the Cistercian Order tried to come to the rescue by purchasing the island in 1925 and sending over two French monks from Thymadeuc to act as bailiffs. The idea was that, after a few years, the Benedictines would make enough money to be able to buy the island back, but in the face of such odds they never had a realistic chance.

One of the Cistercian monks, Fr Corentin Guyader, who was later to be elected as Abbot of Melleraie in Brittany, then took over as Island Steward from Cmdr. Farey.

The price the Cistercians paid for the island was £35,000 and, although this was a considerable increase on what Carlyle had paid for it, such vast sums had been expended during the tenure of the Benedictines that it represented another huge loss.

It is also history how the Benedictines moved to Prinknash in 1928 and the present Community of Cistercians came to Caldey from the Abbey of Notre Dame de Scourmont, near Chimay, in Belgium.

The move to Prinknash was not without its publicity or its moments. Ralph Pomeroy made two lorries available at no cost to the Benedictine Community. It involved a weekly round-trip from October until the end of December, often travelling at night. A raft was devised to get one lorry over to the island. On its journey back to the mainland the raft sank, and the lorry with it. The press, of course, made a meal of it, but considered it to be un-newsworthy that the following day, when the tide receded, the lorry was dried out, started without any trouble and continued on its way to Prinknash.

The move completed, the Benedictines paid warm tribute to 'the two men who have been regularly working for us, Bob Hooper, a Catholic fisherman, and the harbour pilot, William Jones, much better known in Tenby as "Jonah".' Another Jonah. So the names and the families continue. The Prior, Dom Wilfred Upson, also wrote to the Mayor of Tenby, Mr W. H. Thomas, saying, 'Now that our Community has completed its removal from Caldey Island, I feel that I must express to you, and through you to the inhabitants of Tenby, the warmest and most grateful

Hay-making time

thanks of myself and my bretheren for the unfailing kindness which has always been shown to us on every possible occasion by all with whom we have come into contact during the happy years that we lived on the island.

'We shall always remember Tenby and its inhabitants with gratitude, and wish them all prosperity.'

The newcomers, the Cistercians, went off to a much less propitious start. In May of their first year they wrote a disclaimer to the *Tenby Observer* denying rumours that visitors were not welcome on Caldey. It was answered shortly afterwards by a letter paying tribute to the kindness shown by the monks. The whole sad story was to continue for a long time. The trouble was mainly stirred up by an island dweller, Mrs Consuelo King, but that unhappy saga has already been fully chronicled in *Total Community*.

At least one reader asked for any evidence I had that Mrs King 'cultivated' people. I have in my possession a letter which the lady wrote to Amy Mollison when that intrepid aviator was encamped at Pendine in 1933 prior to her Atlantic flight. Mrs King, without any reference to the Prior, was inviting, indeed pleading with, Amy to come to Caldey to stay, and offering all sorts of glittering promises of sandy bays and peace and quiet under the cool monastery walls. But the bit I like best is where she said, 'I think one of your small planes could land at the top of the Island near the Lighthouse or Farm.' That could have been quite interesting.

There was one interesting character on Caldey at that time, of whom little is recorded or remembered, and I am rather sorry about this because I would have liked to know more about him for my own interest. He was the Comte de Ramirez de Arellano de Baceres. Those Tenby people who remember him refer to him as Arellano. The rest of the title would be a challenge for the best. My own interest in him is that he lived in rooms in our house in Saundersfoot, with his secretary, John Francis, and valet, George, whose surname I forget. It was in the early part of 1930 or possibly '31. He claimed to be a cousin of King Alfonso of Spain, but John Craggs, a well-known Tenby character and antique dealer, who was a walking encyclopedia on county families, assured me many years later that Arellano's claims to kinship with the Spanish royal family were strictly bogus.

Our house had not long been built, and my sister and I had laid out what we called a miniature golf-course amongst the ruts and cement in the back yard. The club was an ancient hockey stick and the ball was a cork hockey ball. Arellano played with great fervour and had to be watched carefully if there was the slightest chance of a little quiet cheating. At Easter he gave us each a solid silver egg cup and spoon.

On Caldey he had been living in the house which Aelred Carlyle had built as a guest house. In 1926 the guest house operations were transferred to the mansion at the Priory and Arellano moved in as a tenant for five years at £85 per year with the option to renew for another five years at £100 per year. This much is recorded in the Caldey archives in a document in which the Benedictines explained the background to the letting for the benefit of the Cistercians who were taking over this sitting tenant. The house, they said, had been rented by the Count from Dec. 25th, 1926. The contract was in the name of his mother, 'the Marquesa de Baceras'. The statement then went on to say, 'He wrote in 1928 to say he asked his mother to surrender the lease. His sister (Honourable Mrs Erskine of Mar) wanted him to go back on his decision as she had nowhere to store the furniture.'

Mrs Erskine at that time was renting Trayles, the house on Tenby's Esplanade which had at one time belonged to the larger than life Warren De La Rue, and is now the Atlantic Hotel. Arellano phoned her every day and, with a horror of contamination or infection, always put a piece of toilet paper over the mouthpiece of the old-fashioned set and stood well away from it. Then, of course, he had to shout to make himself heard. What her connection with the house of Mar could have been I do not know, but it is perhaps of interest that Aelred Carlyle's mother also claimed descent from this noble Scottish family. Whether this, or some other, was the reason for Arellano coming to Caldey I have no idea.

He was, of course, a devout Catholic, with a special devotion to St Philomena. He had a life-size statue of her, which lay recumbent on a table below the altar in the room which he had made into a chapel. It was from her that the guest house took its present name of St Philomena's.

St Philomena was an adolescent girl and the statue, which was in our house for a while after Arellano left Caldey, was very beautiful. Her story is not relevant here except to say that in 1961 the pertinent authority in Rome ordered her feast day to be discontinued, the shrine at Muguano to be dismantled, and her name expunged from any calendar in which it appeared. She, too, it seems was just a trifle bogus.

The Count also had in his bedroom a wealth of candles, incense, rosaries, crucifixes and relics, including a part of the Cross on which Our Lord was crucified. I believe it is generally acknowledged that if all the true relics of the Cross were collected together in one place there would be enough to build a mighty cathedral.

When he left us he went to live for a time at Orielton, near Pembroke, (shades of Col. Saurin and Gramfer) which he rented from the late T. W. Colley of Pembroke. This well-known character, a builders' merchant, had bought Orielton for the timber in its woods, and my father, who had much dealing with him, effected the introduction which led to Arellano going to live there. I remember visiting him at Orielton and being treated to a demonstration on how to shoot pheasants. He would place some food on the lawn to attract them, then retire to the house and shoot them through the bedroom window. It was not the way I had been taught, but maybe things are different in Spain.

The general idea in the area was that Arellano and his entourage were drowned on their way to America in the early days of the war when the boat on which they were travelling was sunk. There was strict censorship of news at that time, and all sorts of rumours and counter-rumours were rife. Be that as it may, it was the last that was heard of him. If I have written of him at greater length than is warranted it is only because I seem to have remembered more about him than any of those whom I have questioned.

Dom Wilfred Upson had succeeded Dom Aelred as Abbot and, when the guest house was transferred to the old Priory mansion, it was run for a while by two of the McHardy girls. Veronica married Joe Barrett, who for many years looked after the lighthouse, and Mary married Peter Wire, the son of the Benedictines; aptly named electrician. Another sister, Cecilia, had already married Valentine Kilbride, who had come to teach the monks weaving, and had set up his operations in the old sanctuary over the Priory. They became engaged three weeks after their first meeting. Then Dom Wilfred's sister took over. The house was damp, sparsely furnished and in poor shape generally. In 1930, Miss Upson went to live at St Philomena's, and three ladies, the sisters Misses Grossé, aunts to one of the monks at Chimay, came from Belgium in 1930 to run it. They were to remain on the island for more than thirty years, and two of them died there and are buried in St David's churchyard. During those years they became very much a part of the island as did others who were there at the time. And, as always, life was never without its lighter side. Take, for example, a Special St Samson's Day Issue of *The Caldey Gossiper* in 1931. One news item is headed 'The War on Caldey' and reads, 'The punitive expedition against the colony of rats inhabitating (sic) that part of the Island known as "Timbercote", is meeting with success. Already the rebels have suffered severe losses, thanks to the fine gunnery of Dick Cummins. It has not yet been ascertained whether the rebels' ringleader, Peter, is still at large, but he has not been seen lately. It may be he is collecting reinforcements. For the benefit of visitors it should be stated that for years this colony of rats has, until recently, lived peaceably on the best chicken food. Not content with this luxurious life, they suddenly commence devouring the chickens also. This we think a bit thick. Hence the declaration of war.'

There was much of the same nature, and it was sad that one person, as so often happens in life, could have caused so much trouble. Mrs King had active help in her campaign from a journalist on the *Western Mail*, J. C. Griffith Jones. In later years he contributed to a paper for which I was a staff writer, but suffice it to say he was never one whose company I sought. This story, too, has already been sufficiently chronicled, including the presence on the island of the four little Ethiopian children, members of Emperor Haile Selassie's family. One of them was little Prince Iskundra, son of Ras Desta.

It was in the midst of all this that Geoffrey Hoare's book, *Caldey, Isle of the Severn Sea*, was published. A highly skilled photographer, he was a good friend of the Benedictines and the Cistercians, and the last thing that he would have wished would have been to hurt either of them. But, coming in the midst of all the contention and the trouble being fomented, his reference to a German submarine during the first war was of no help at all. People suddenly remembered the silly rumours of twenty years previously.

Visiting the island at the same time as the children of the Ethiopian royal family he was able to take a delightful picture of Iskundra.

In 1939 St Joseph's, or the Barracks, at the edge of the Common, was pulled down, another era had come to an end, and another war had started.

Prince Iskundra of Abysinnia   *G. G. Hoare*

Chapter 18

The graveyard

How much more would it be possible to write of those who have moved through the pages of the history of Caldey? Much has long since been forgotten and, of that which remains, it would be impossible to tell it all. Many fine words have been penned by those who have pondered awhile by the mute, yet eloquent, headstones in country churchyards. Thomas Gray, with his immortal *Elegy*, was one of them. Richard Jefferies, more than a hundred years ago, in *Hodge and his Masters*, wrote, 'Hodge died, and the very grave-digger grumbled as he delved through the earth hard-bound in the iron frost, for it jarred his hand and might break his spade. The low mound will soon be level, and the place of his burial shall not be known.'

There were many such mounds on Caldey which, in time, once more became level above generations of unknown Hodges— Webbs, and James, and Matthews, and Rowes and all the rest of them. Some such thought must have been in the mind of an anonymous contributor to *Pax* who, in 1919, wrote, 'All memory of the dead had disappeared from our village churchyard when first we came to Caldey: it was a bare, open field, called in the maps "Church Park", exposed to the four winds of heaven. Now it is a little God's acre, enclosed on each side by tall fuchsia hedges: and the years which have gone by have left records of their passing in the little crosses that mark the graves of the islanders who have gone home.'

But, in time, even the crosses will perish, and the faded names with them.

Whose, then, were those which, as yet, have some mark by which they and their stories may be recalled? In the ossuary in the corner are the remains of some of the unknown, collected and placed together. On those there can only be speculation.

In the next grave was buried young Arthur Coe, aged fifteen, in 1908. And now nobody seems to know anything about little

Arthur. So what was his story? Does the occasional day visitor in summer coming over on one of the boats in the Pool ever give the inscription a glance and wonder?

It was a little before midnight on a Saturday evening in that summer of 1908 that a lad from the farm burst into the old cottage monastery, sobbing and beside himself with grief. He shared the Well-house with little Arthur Coe, whose father had recently given him a gun as a birthday present. Not knowing the gun was loaded, the poor lad had picked it up and the trigger went off. Arthur was killed instantaneously. The lad was not named, and perhaps it was as well. It must have been a cruel burden for him to carry through life.

Next to Arthur was another lad, who died not two years later, before he had reached the age of fifteen. Willie John Matthews was the grandson of old John and Hannah Matthews. The inscription on her cross says that her name was Anna, but the 1881 *Census Returns* say that it was Hannah and that she came from Castlemartin. Her husband came from neighbouring Bosherston, and they were amongst those who were received into the Catholic Church at the time of the conversion on Caldey. They were married for fifty-four years.

Willie John died of septicaemia, and his father, John, who was present at his death, was given as a collier of Pontycymmer, near Bridgend. Like so many others in those hard times he would no doubt have gone away to the valleys to look for work. They did that sort of thing in those days. And then no doubt he would have come back to Caldey when Carlyle made his attempt to revive the quarry industry, for that was where Jack Matthews died. He would have been forty-six at the time.

In the lovely month of May it was that he was killed. A blast of powder had not fired, 'and bending over it he received the full charge of it right into himself, and his poor body was carried down, scorched and scarred and mangled, from the shelf up on the cliff where his summons had come.'

There is no inscription to say so, but he was buried in the same grave as his son, Willie John.

It was when I was looking at the next cross that one of the monks came along and I offered some deep line of thought on the imponderables of life and death, and he nudged me in the ribs with his elbow, chuckled, and said, 'Go on, move over.' I rather like the monks' attitude to death.

The cross in question marked the resting place of Michael Cooke, aged twenty-six, who died in 1912. In the register it says that he was a male hospital nurse, so what was he doing to have been buried on Caldey?

In his earlier days he had been a novice with the Benedictines at Painsthorpe before ever they came to Caldey. He found his true vocation eventually as a sick-berth attendant in the Royal Navy and became a Catholic before the Benedictines did. Eventually he contracted consumption, and he came back to find a home with his old Community amongst whom he died. He had been receiving the sacraments regularly from the parish priest in Tenby, Fr Carew, who buried him. It was probably the first Catholic ceremony of a public nature on the island since the days of Henry VIII, for it was six months before the Benedictines were received into the Catholic Church.

Next to Michael comes old John Webb whose story we already know. But who was Thomas Cleary lying next to him?

There is an interesting report of his passing. It says of him:

> Dear old Thomas Cleary, most faithful of retainers, what a shock it was, at Candlemas in 1916, when he fell dead at the landing slip down in Priory Bay. He had been with us for many years; and in the old railway train at Painsthorpe, which served as a noviciate, an overflow of the guest-house, a poultry food store and what not, he occupied the end carriage, and spent his days chiefly in the making of fishing gimp. At Caldey he looked after the tiny tin store, before the present shop was built. His pride in it was very real, and great was his fury one day when an Islander remarked, 'Oh yes, it is a great convenience having a shop on the Island, for you can always run in for a penny-worth of salt or such like if there is anything you've forgotten to bring over from Tenby.'

He liked to recall how once he helped King Edward, then Prince of Wales, take off his hat and coat; and one of his most cherished possessions was a passport which he carried with him when he visited the battlefields after the Franco-German War of 1870. Dickens was

Thomas Cleary

his great joy, and indeed, little old-fashioned gentleman, he himself might have stepped out of his favourite author's pages. A pinch of good snuff—Kendal Brown for preference—a musical box, and his bright red socks (he would rarely appear in public with hose of any other colour) are three things that associate themselves with his memory—little details that stand out, together with lovable traits of his character, his devotion especially and his complete trustworthiness.

Some of the other names are already familiar but, further along the line, comes Emma McEntee. It is worth remembering her story, if only as a warning to those who do foolish things still. 'Some are wise,' the seer said, 'and some are otherwise.'

Emma lived on Caldey and, in the merry month of May in the year 1924, her friend, Miss Trusty, came to stay with her. And they went for a picnic on St Margaret's on a Sunday afternoon in that merry month of May, which is a tempting thing to do, but not particularly wise unless you know what you are doing. And, on the way back, they found a fierce-running channel of tide ahead of them, and then, when they turned to go back, they found another fierce-running channel of tide behind them. And so they were drowned. And Miss Trusty's body was never found, but Emma's was washed up at Freshwater and buried in St David's. It would be nice to think it could at least serve as a warning to others, but I doubt it.

Ethel Harris, Dom Aseph's sister, who was living at Tŷ Gwyn, was drowned, too. A search party failed to find her and her body was washed up some days later at Pembrey, near Burry Port. That was in 1927.

The question of drowning also comes to mind with the names on another cross, and little enough in the records, to tell of it. It is just that I happen to know.

John Dolby was a novice on Caldey with the Benedictines. Although he had lost one hand he was a carpenter of considerable ability and was called on to help the Tenby painter and decorator, James Thomas, who was doing some work up at the farmhouse on the island. When the Benedictines moved to Prinknash John Dolby went with them, but he never really settled. For one thing, because of the physical disability which would have prevented his handling the host at Communion, he knew he could never become a priest, and he wrote to ask Stanley Thomas, James's son, to find him a job and lodgings in Tenby. For a time he lived with Stanley and his wife, and worked for Stanley's father, who was again working on the island, probably at St Philomena's for Arellano. After a while the Cistercians offered him a job, and he moved back to Caldey.

Occasionally he would come across to Tenby to spend the week-end with Stanley and his wife. When he acquired a dog he used to bring it with him and board it for the weekend at the kennels at Zion House, at the end of The Croft, where there is now a block of flats. It was not long before he married the kennel-maid. They lived at Green Pastures.

It was in the winter of 1945, if I remember correctly, that Frances Dolby disappeared one evening, and the following morning her body was washed up by the Black Rock on the beach beyond Amroth. I was one of those who helped to carry her up to the New Inn. It was assumed that she had gone for a walk or to collect driftwood on the rocks and had perhaps slipped.

It was not long after this that John advertised for a wife. From the applications he received he drew up a short list of three and went off to interview the first one. Her name was Gertrude, and she agreed to come to Caldey for a month's trial, with her mother as chaperon. She became the second Mrs Dolby. She remained on the island until her final illness, in 1971, when she died in Swansea, but she either lacked sympathy with the monks or an understanding of their problems. I used to meet her occasionally at the house of mutual friends in Tenby. At that time Br Thomas had asked me about selling them a Guernsey bull calf, to rear as a stock bull, as they were thinking in terms of improving the quality of the milk. Gertrude got to hear of it and said, 'And you be sure to charge them plenty. They're rolling in money over there and pleading poverty all the time.'

What it shows I don't know, but it must show something, for it was in the 1950s, when the Caldey Community were still losing money, being subsidised by the mother house in Chimay, and were in fact under threat of being closed down unless they could at least break even. And I mention the episode only because of this.

When she died she was buried on Caldey, and when John died, two years later, at the age of eighty-six, at the old people's home at Pembroke, he was cremated and his ashes buried with her.

Amidst the crosses there is at least one other case of drowning, and of much more recent date. In 1977 six years old Teresa Biggs was staying with her grandparents at St Philomena's when she went with a picnic party to the lovely, but deadly, Sandtop Bay. It is a beautiful bay, but highly dangerous for bathing. I reckoned I could swim a bit at one time, but I would not feel safe there even paddling. The much-loved little Teresa went into the water unobserved, and there are usually flowers on the cross which marks the place where she went so early to her rest, amongst others who were spared to enjoy Caldey for many decades, such as

Little Beryl Fogwell (left), with her sister, a few days before she was burned to
death   G. G. Hoare

dear old John Judkins and his wife, Edith Alis-Smith who was
eighty-eight, and Alice Harris who was eighty nine.

There is no cross in the churchyard, but there was another
tragedy in the winter of 1935 when little four year old Beryl

Fogwell, grandchild of Sam Fogwell, who had died in 1926, was burned to death. A Tenby doctor had been taken across by the Tenby lifeboat in mountainous seas, but it was to no avail and she died in Tenby hospital the same night.

So the list could go on, some of them whose ages are not recorded, but whose names and memories are cherished amongst the islanders.

Epitomising it all perhaps is the account of the burial of Beatrice Bowes, the mother of one of the Benedictines, who died in 1919. The report says:

> On Mothering Sunday, after a long and painful illness bravely borne, Mrs Bowes died very peacefully during Vespers: and on March 31st was laid to rest in the village churchyard. Her son, Dom Samson, in the midst of his monastic Brethren sang the Requiem Mass: and chanting *In Paradisum* we accompanied him to his mother's grave. A lovely spring morning, the Island was looking its fairest: earth and sky and ocean were proclaimed aloud, for all to hear, the note of Peace. The Italian-blue sea, flecked by the shadows of great billowy clouds and the russet and white of little sailing craft, was linked up with the purple of the newly ploughed fields by the grey cliffs and the thin green of the sedge-grass on the sand-dunes; and the snow-clad Preceley mountains reared their crests away over in the far corner of the county. The scene was dappled by the snowy white of the seagulls as they wheeled about in their flight; and a lark sang overhead. Amidst so much beauty, and the fragrance of Masses and prayers, the mother of a monk was buried. Of those who stood around there was none to whom the wish did not come that his own ending might be as this.
>
> *Sit in pace locus eorum et habitatio eorum in sancta Sion.*

Chapter 19

Monastic characters

The story of the war years on Caldey has already been told, together with the progress of the Cistercian community and the commercial developments there up to the 1970s.

I made the point at the beginning that, when *Total Community* was published, there were those who expressed disappointment that I had not written more about the people who had been involved and wrestled for a living on the island over the years. By now it should be evident why it would have been more than difficult to know where to begin to incorporate such a wealth of material in a work which was essentially about the monastic community. And, even then, I had not written in as much detail as I could have done.

The former Abbot, Dom James Wicksteed, who gave me so much help in the work, and showed so much kindness, also discouraged too much identifying of individuals. It was part of the monastic way of life, in the jargon of the day, to keep a low profile. And, of course, I respected that wish, using such expressions as 'one of the monks told me.'

But who, of all the visitors who came to know and love dear old Fr Anselm in the years when he was deputy guest-master, could not hear his droll voice saying, in reply to my question about some monk or other 'swiping a book', 'It's what we call Total Community'? Hence the title of the book.

And, who, of all those who have laughed with Fr Bernard, the parish priest, could not hear him, in that same book, as, in his attitude to death, he spoke of 'a corpse being lugged about the place' and a box instead of a coffin? He it was who nudged me in the ribs and said, 'Go on, move over'. I said to the Abbot once that maybe Fr Bernard had missed his vocation and should have been on the stage at the London Palladium, and the Abbot said, 'He probably was for all I know'. Yet it was Fr Bernard also whom I quoted, with his joyful attitude to death being, not an end, but a mere beginning leading on to something far greater, as he then went on to reel off the great passage from Paul's letter to the Thessalonians, 'I would not have you to be ignorant, brethren, concerning them which are asleep . . .'

This question of anonymity also applied until more recent years to the question of photography. Time was when monks were not supposed to have their pictures taken without prior permission, which is not intended as a pun. Maybe it was this which influenced Dom Wicksteed's attitude to photography generally. Marvellously cooperative and helpful though he was in every other way, he saw no point in having a group picture taken of the Community to bring the record up to date, and there are several gaps in their pictorial records over the last twenty years or so. On the other hand, Fr Dominic, who died in 1980, and who had come over with the first contingent from Chimay in 1928, was an enthusiastic, if not highly skilled, photographer. And, in the earlier years, the camera he used was not all that good. But he left behind, not hundreds, but literally thousands of negatives of snaps, which are of great benefit to the Community as well as interest. He even took photographs of the pipes when drains were being laid, and the information contained in such pictures can readily be appreciated by those who have ever suffered the problems of drain trouble. How truly it has been said that a picture is worth a thousand words. He always took pictures before, during and after any building work that was being done, and there are islanders who insist that he would have had even more and better pictures if he had always remembered to put a film in the camera.

Apart from the help of such a pictorial record which this gentle, cheerful man bequeathed, I am bound to have a soft spot for him, because it was his knowledge which led me eventually to the old monastery Journal which had lain forgotten under a thirty year layer of dust until, with the help of the Abbot, I tracked it down. At the time I suggested that the Journal had been written up at various stages from other records, and also wondered why Fr Bertin had ceased to keep the record a couple of years before he

The burned-out monastery church, 1949, and repair work underway in 1950
(see *Total Community*, pub. Five Arches Press, Tenby)

Mass being said in the ruins of the burned-out church.

died. I know the answer now because, since then, I have discovered in the monastery's archives the penny exercise books in which he had made his notes, right up to the end, ready to enter them in the Journal.

Not only was Fr Dominic the official photographer but he was, amongst other things, the baker. I said he was cheerful. And cheerful people tend to sing. The only problem was that dear old Dominic, in his last years, had become stone deaf, and that presented a problem for the others when he was singing, to his own time and his own tune, in choir. Of recent years the monks took a serious look at their future path to see whether there were any ways in which they ought to reorganise their services of worship and their ways of community life. At the bottom of each questionnaire was a space for suggestions. One brother, and I recognised the writing, had written, 'Persuade Rent-A-Tenor to take on our Rank-Hovis Caruso otherwise any of above improve-

The snow lay deep and white—John Bates' house, now demolished, c.1952

ments likely to be nullified and our removal to St David's *en bloc* only a matter of time.'

For posterity, and the benefit of other than locals, be it recorded that St David's in this case refers to what used to be known as the asylum at Carmarthen.

Towards the end of his time 'Fr Dom's' baking prowess had declined a little. He had gone off to Swansea for an operation, when his eyesight was failing, and I met Josh Richards, the plumber, one day in Tenby. He, too, had worked with my father when he was younger, but for many years later in life his little Charlie Chaplin figure had been a familiar part of the scene on Caldey where he must have known every tap and grease trap and 'S' bend. We usually had a chat about the island on such occasions and on this one, in his humorous way, he opined that they would have to do something over there before long otherwise they would be out of flour. The Abbot, apparently, had taken

An unusual scene

It's not always either solemn or old, 1951

And the band played on, 1949

The play is the thing, 1951

Who is this Danny La Rue? 1952

Josh Richards (left)

over in the bakery during 'Fr Dom's' absence and the bread was 'lovely and fluffy' but 'Fr Dom's' bread always presented Josh with no small problem when it came to chewing it.

There are so many such stories which could be told, because there is a marvellous rapport between individual monks and various employees of the Community and other local people who come in contact with its members. And, of course, the Community have long been working towards Christian unity in the area they have made their home. This being so, especially since Fr Dominic and Fr Aelred died within four months of each other in 1980, some mention should also be made of this other rather remarkable member of the Community.

Born Alfred Williams, Fr Aelred spoke who-knows-how-many languages. Not only many European tongues, but also with a specialised familiarity with Mandarin, Cantonese, Japanese and several Chinese dialects. In Hong-Kong he had been a professor of English, no doubt owing his knowledge of Japanese to his

Fr Aelred Williams in characteristic attitude

having remained in Hong-Kong throughout the Japanese occupation of the islands during the war. Of him it could well have been said that his slogan was, 'Become a monk and see the world,' for he travelled much on monastic affairs.

It was in 1951 that he wrote to the then Prior of Caldey, Dom Albert Derzelle, saying, 'I am a Welshman who wants to be a monk. As Caldey is the only Cistercian monastery in Wales I should like to become a member of your community.' The letter came all the way from Hong-Kong and, when he arrived, it was discovered that he had the rare mixture of Celtic volatility and Oriental impassiveness. How he came to be in Hong-Kong I am not quite sure, but I can account for his family background because he told the story with great delight the last time he stayed a couple of nights with us. His Nonconformist father was a schoolmaster from either Montgomeryshire or Merioneth. I can't remember which. His mother was a Hong-Kong Portugese and a staunch Catholic. Upon their marriage, the husband promised that any children should be brought up as Catholics. So when the first child arrived it was duly baptised into the Catholic church.

When the second one arrived, however, the father thought about things, and the good Welsh Nonconformist soul of him rebelled. He saw no reason why the Pope should have all his family and, promise or not, he insisted that the second child should be brought up as a Nonconformist.

Greatly distressed, the mother took her troubles to the priest. He would seem to have been an enlightened man, well ahead of his time. He told her that she must not destroy her marriage over such an issue, but to continue to be a good wife and mother and take it to the Lord in prayer.

When the third child arrived the father said it would be all right for the Pope to have that one, but, when the fourth came, that was one for the chapel. The fifth went to the Pope, the sixth to the Nonconformists. The seventh, which was the last, was one for the Pope. And then, Aelred concluded the tale with great pleasure, on his death-bed his father was received into the Catholic church.

During his twenty-seven years as one of Caldey's monastic community Fr Aelred acted as secretary to the Abbot and to the Trustees. He taught philosophy and he edited, almost from its inception, *Cistercian Studies*, which involved corresponding with contributors and subscribers in many parts of the world, as often as not in their native language. As a matter of routine, and with typical thoroughness, he daily cleaned the monastery's WC's and washrooms. And he was always ready to give a haircut to any member of the Community who required the service. Small wonder, after his death from a coronary thrombosis at the early age of sixty-four, one of the brothers said of him, 'He was, it is true, given an alarm clock, but what he really needed was time.'

A note on him in the Caldey archives says, 'He is greatly missed. We shall not see his like again.' He was indeed a lovely, warm personality, and a man of vast Christian conviction.

It was in 1951, when Alfred Williams, subsequently Fr Aelred, applied to enter the Community, that the other Aelred, formerly Benjamin Fearnley Carlyle, came back to Caldey for the last time. And, of course, Fr Dominic took a picture of him. He had also visited the island in 1948. Following his last visit he wrote to the

Prior and said, 'Caldey must always be one of the dearest places on earth to me, for there I rejoiced and suffered; and I don't think that even you can quite understand how much that recent visit of a few days meant to me . . .'

Much had been made of him on this occasion, but the adulation did not meet with unanimous approval for there were those who were not without their misgivings. Fr Patrick Rafferty, a single-minded individual, wrote to the Abbot General of the Order expressing his displeasure. Dom Aelred Carlyle died four years later and was buried at Prinknash alongside so many of the Community he had founded.

When *Total Community* was published there were a few critics who said that I had based my assessment of Carlyle entirely on what Peter Anson had written. Apart from the fact that it matters little what critics say, this was not so. I could well have been wrong in my assessment. That is not for me to say. But my opinions were based on many things, including local knowledge,

Dom Aelred Carlyle on his last visit to Caldey, 1951

other than Peter Anson's writings, and they were, and remain, opinions honestly formed and still held.

Perhaps the saddest thing of all is that there are those who believe they can obliterate Carlyle's faults by painting all of him white. But there are three things which must for ever be marked up against his name as substantial credits.

The Community which he founded still flourishes at Prinknash.

Perhaps most important of all, he found his true niche later in life in Canada where he did such work of real Christian charity and compassion that, whoever is on duty when he rings the bell at the Pearly Gates, will assuredly say, 'Come in'.

And, without what he did at Caldey, what has been done since would not have been possible.

With the wisdom which cometh with hindsight we can look back and realise, with the hymnist, that God moves in a mysterious way his wonders to perform.

Blessing of the new boat, 1950

Corpus Christi, 1953

Bede Camm, who had much to do with the earlier Community and knew something of their problems, wrote, 'If we cannot honestly speak well of them then it would be better to be silent and to pray for them.' Like Done Bushell we can be positive and praise the good.

The ultimate aim of all of us is to get to Heaven, although we all travel by slightly different routes. As long as we get there eventually is all that matters. And even Paul, indeed especially Paul, did not get off to a very promising start. All that, however, is forgotten, as it should be, in the knowledge that he got there in the end. Aelred Carlyle, after all life's vicissitudes, and in due season, will have followed him.

Br Joachim

The actor Rupert Davies with Fr Anthony Ffrench-Mullen who were prisoners-of-war together (see *Total Community*)

Fr Thaddeus with visiting orphans, 1970

Chapter 20

More days of change

Just as Simon Kidney went to Caldey as a coastguard during the War to end wars, and stayed on to work for the Benedictines, so Jack 'New Inn' went there as a coastguard during the War to end aggression, and stayed on to work for the Cistercians. For good measure he married Teresa Styles, whose mother had cooked for the men at the Barracks. They were married by Teresa's brother, Dom Alberic Styles, a member of the Benedictine community at Prinknash, who was subsequently tragically killed in a car smash. The Styles were another well-known Caldey family, but Teresa was the only one who stayed on after marrying. She and Jack lived up at the farm-house, known as St Illtud's.

Although Jack was known on the island by his real name of Jack Davies, I have written of him as Jack 'New Inn' because I never knew him or heard him spoken of by any other name. If ever a man was bred right for island life it must have been Jack, because his whole life up to the time he went to Caldey was what those who know no better would have regarded as the backwoods. A tall, strong man, he lived near us at Amroth at the New Inn with his aged parents when that hostelry was like something of which we once read long ago but never encountered. This is not the time or place to embark upon an essay on the subject but, in 1928, an application was made by the police to Whitland magistrates to close the New Inn. Not because of any late hours, rowdyism or any of the antics of which we read when such applications are made these days. In this instance the application was being made because, the police said, trade was so poor the place was not needed and 'the sanitary conditions were generally poor'. Typically, there was a small farm attached. The police gave the figures for the stock as 'one horse, four cows, some sheep and some pigs'. The figures for the bar trade were even more revealing. Old John Davies was selling two gallons of beer a week, one bottle of spirits a month and six bottles of stout a week. Happy days.

201

Everything stops for tea—Jack Davies, 1949

The probable truth of the matter was that New Inn, tucked away in the far corner of Carmarthenshire, just over the border from Pembrokeshire, was a bit of a problem for the Carmarthen police who would have harrassed a few harmless cases of drinking after shut-tap with the same brave enthusiasm as their successors of today's generation in panda cars scull around the rural areas, where the local police stations have been closed down, in search of criminal motorists with faulty rear lights. Happy to relate, the magistrates declined to accede to the police request.

Jack was to remain on Caldey until the end of his time. He and Teresa died within weeks of each other in 1963. She was so ill that she was not told that Jack had gone on ahead of her. He had no religious conviction and once, when asked where he thought he would go after he died, he replied in his usual jocular manner, 'Well, wherever I go, there'll be plenty of others there for company.'

Teresa, a devout Catholic, was buried on the island, but Jack was laid to rest alongside his parents and younger brother at Marros, across the bay from Caldey. He had lived on the island long enough to witness something of the progress of civilisation. In 1938 the submarine telephone cable was broken, and the island was without telephonic communication until a radiotelephone system was installed by the G.P.O. as an experiment in 1951. A new cable was subsequently laid, and more recently the system has been improved so that more of the islanders have been able to have the telephone installed.

In 1965 an underwater electricity cable brought the benefit of mains electricity to the island, and the former lime-kiln changed the face of things once more when it was incorporated for use as a sub-station.

Not that everything was progress and building up. Change is written on all earthly things. In the winter of 1954 Pembrokeshire experienced the full fury of an Atlantic hurricane. It took the roof off the old farmhouse on Skomer and inflicted further damage to the rapidly deteriorating mansion up at the Priory. Two of the Grossé sisters died, and were buried on the island, but the third went back to Belgium. By the 1970s the mansion had become unsafe and was pulled down, to leave behind only a few pictures and the many stories of those who had lived there for more than a century and a half.

The guest house activities were again moved back to St Philomena's and, in 1968, this was extended to accommodate twenty-four people. One of the monks has always been in charge as guest-master but, in 1972, a steward and his wife arrived.

Zdzislaw Sieroslawski had made a career in the Polish Air Force. A prisoner-of-war in Russia, two years in Siberia, he came to this country in 1941 and joined the R.A.F. He met his wife, Jo-Jo, when she was in the W.A.A.F. Although his name was pronounced as it was spelt he became known to an ever growing host of friends as Zed.

His wife's name was really Josephine, but to the hundreds who have come to the island and have cause to be grateful for her many kindnesses she has always been, and always will be, just Jo-Jo.

After the war they farmed in west Wales for more than twenty years. One of their boys used to go to Caldey to camp. Jo-Jo met the Abbot and asked whether they could live on Caldey. And so, for nine years, until 1981, they ran Philomena's and became an integral part of island life. Zed was a familiar figure at Compline, a service which he loved.

Writing of this service early this century the Rev E. Hermitage Day said:

> Compline is the solemn commendation of the Community to the loving care of its Lord for the night. The intention and spirit of Compline are well interpreted by an unknown writer of the fifteenth century, who wrote for the Brigittine Nuns of Sion an exposition of their Office. 'Compline,' he says, 'is the seventh and the last hour of divine Service, and it is as much to say as a fulfilling, for in the end thereof the seven hours of Divine Service are fulfilled. And therewith also are ended and fulfilled speaking, eating and drinking, and labouring, and all bodily businesses. So that after that time ought to be kept great stillness and strait silence, not only from words, but also from all noises and deeds save only privy and soft prayer, and holy thinking and bodily sleep. For Compline betokeneth the end of man's life or the end of the world, when the chosen of our Lord shall be delivered from all travail and woe, and be brought to endless quiet and rest. And therefore each person ought to dispose him to bedward, as if his bed were his grave'.

Zed was on his knees in prayer at Compline when those around him realised that he had been called to higher spheres. He would have wanted it no other way, and he was laid to rest in the same grave as his little grand-daughter, Teresa Biggs.

Jo-Jo remained on the island and it was then that Andy McHardy and Sally came to take over at Philomena's and cement still further the family ties with Caldey.

There is a good family atmosphere at Philomena's, and all that is asked of visitors is that they should help with the washing-up, laying of tables after meals and by making their own beds. On the other hand, it is stressed that those who are fortunate enough to be able to avail themselves of this hospitality are expected to have a serious, religious purpose in mind, even if it is only to take full

Andy McHardy with his wife, mother and family

advantage of rest and quiet for reflection. It is no place for a holiday with transistors.

For some years the guest rooms attached to the monastery were also open to visiting friends of both sexes. Now, however, these quarters are confined to the use of men and youths who wish to have a closer experience of monastic life, possibly sometimes with the thought of seeking a vocation.

The bedrooms are simply furnished, and comfortable, each with a wash-basin and hot and cold water. One special room with an alcove also has a WC. Not surprisingly it is known as Waterloo. And still there are those, who know nothing about monks, who believe they must be very dour and serious types without any sense of humour.

Their sense of being not entirely unaware of what is going on in the world also extends to the installation of a video recorder for their television set. This may not have been a unanimous choice. Before they had the video they were able to watch the recorded rugby programmes on Sunday afternoons in winter. And with rugby being the second religion in Wales, this was perhaps no bad thing for the religious to do in the land of their adoption. Sunday afternoon is about the only time they watch television. With the coming of the video it has meant that they are now able to select certain higher-minded programmes during the week to watch them on Sunday.

There is, of course, so much which could be written of such a place at any one time, with people and customs changing as they do. What is well-known and obvious to us today may be ommitted. Yet future generations would probably thank us for having left some record of it. Frequently when reading that which was written by those who visited the island years ago I have found myself wishing they had been more specific and written in more detail on many points.

How much, for example, could be written about the shipwrecks which have happened round Caldey's rugged cliffs over the centuries? Yet little of it has been recorded and, handed down by word of mouth, is eventually forgotten.

In the early part of the century, for example, the isolated stack of rock standing out from the headland facing St Margaret's was known to the older inhabitants as Frenchman's island. Covered with the greenest of turf it is made more beautiful in spring by the thrift or 'sea-pink'. The story went that early in the previous century, one morning after a heavy storm, some of the islanders who were out that way were astonished to see a number of men on the islet. They were French sailors, whose ship had been wrecked during the gale, and they had been thrown up there. One of them had died during the night and it was said that he had been buried there.

Peter Anson told a story of how he was in Hull addressing a

meeting of the Society of St Vincent de Paul on the need for work among Catholic seamen. He was one of the founders of the Apostleship of the Sea. On that occasion a merchant seaman came up to him and said, 'I heard the Canon say you were from Caldey when he gave out the notices at Mass this morning, so I've come along this afternoon. I was wrecked on Caldey sixteen years ago, in a coaster. We swam ashore and the people were very kind to us. You're the first person from Caldey I've spoken to since.'

So, from here on perhaps I should try to record something of that which will help to bring the record up to date.

Chapter 21

The material and the spiritual

In 1980 Dom James Wicksteed resigned as Abbot. He had completed twenty-one years as Abbot, during which time he had carried a heavy burden of responsibility. It was a great loss to the Community, for he was a man of vast intellect and prodigious physical endurance. This, perhaps, was his weakness, because whenever a monk was ill, or failing, the Abbot, in his belief that he should lead by example rather than precept, would take on the extra duty himself, as witness the occasion when he took over as baker in place of the absent Fr Dominic.

As time went by, with members of the Community growing older and sometimes infirm, with no young recruits coming forward, and the occasional death depleting their ranks, it will be readily understood that the Abbot's task, as he saw it, must have seemed daunting. I wrote in *Total Community*, 'It is not unusual for men to follow other vocations in life and then change to something else, and it is no different for a monk. When he changes his mind it does not necessarily make him any worse as a man or lacking as a Christian.' There is no harm in repeating that. Nor is there any harm in repeating the fact that I also said if God wanted monasticism to continue He would no doubt show the way to those who would follow it. It was in the second edition of *The Sounds Between* that I wrote, 'The work of the earlier monks in spreading Christianity and carrying the message is now perhaps outdated, but it would be difficult to argue that the world is no longer in need of prayer.'

The ideal number of monks for Caldey would probably be something like forty, to enable them to do all the work themselves, as they would wish. There is the farm work, the gardening, care of the woodlands, maintenance of the buildings and field walls, as well as the making of perfume and chocolate, and odd side lines for which individual members have a certain aptitude, such as wood-turning or stone-polishing. And this is not to mention

The Cistercian Community, 1983

catering for the needs of daily visitors throughout the summer holiday season.

Instead of forty, as it once was, the number has now been reduced to twelve. And of these Br James is 'on loan' from Chimay. But as he has been on Caldey, apart from the odd break, for more than thirty years, the chances are that he could stay. It is what is known as *tempus non definitum*. What Caldey would do without him is difficult to imagine.

During the winter months he does a tremendous amount of work with the tractor and concrete mixer, keeping the jetty and walls in good repair, and effecting improvements generally in that area. He grows watercress in two of the mediaeval ponds. He works in the garden. He collects stones and polishes and sets them. In his spare time he indulges in one of his hobbies, which is archaeological digging.

It is fitting that he will have been the cause of setting a little poser for archaeologists yet to be. Disposal of rubbish on the island has always been something of a problem, and for many years much of it has been dumped over the cliffs above Redberry Bay on the seaward side of the island. The philosophy is probably a case of 'out of sight, out of mind'. On one occasion it was the cause of some little embarassment to the late Br Thomas. On the death of one of the islanders a cottage had to be cleared out. Most householders, and certainly those who have ever had to move, will know how rubbish can accumulate over the years. To Br Thomas's lot that time fell the task of getting rid of a motley collection of cracked jugs and chamber pots, iron bedsteads and at least one old horse-hair mattress. By way of a change he thought they might be less of an eyesore if he dumped them at sea and, with this in mind, he put the whole lot aboard the boat with which his name will always be synonymous, the *Lollipop*.

He duly jetisoned his cargo, and the water round Caldey is very deep in places. Everything gurgled its way beautifully into the azure depths as planned, with the exception of the wretched horse-hair mattress which, with a nicely flowing tide and fresh north-westerly breeze behind it, immediately set course for the area round the High Cliff, in full view of Tenby across the water.

As luck would have it, there was a report abroad that a yacht had got into some difficulties across Carmarthen Bay in the area of Burry Port and the notorious Cefn Sidan sand bar. It was some time since there had been any sighting of her and people were on the look-out. People included an enthusiastic young newspaper reporter in Tenby who espied what looked to him very much like a mattress drifting roung High Cliff point. When he phoned Caldey it was Br Thomas who answered him.

No, Brother hadn't seen anything of a missing yacht. Eventually the reporter said, 'Well, where do you think the mattress belongs, Brother?'

'Oh,' said Brother, 'on the sea-bed I should think.'

The confusion caused by Br James will be of a more lasting character. Once upon a time there were three blowholes, out to the west of the island, above the Cathedral Caves. Now there are not.

Br Thomas receives a visit from his mother and aunt

The caves have been much written about. There are five altogether, and the largest is a vast affair, longer than the nave of Westminster Cathedral. Perhaps the blowholes have been written about even more than the caves. They have certainly been of more concern to the Community. These yawning holes, in the land well away from the cliff, have always been a temptation to those who would throw stones to find out what sort of noise would come up from the bottom. Should there have been somebody down below at the time, exploring the caves, the noise could have been considerable. And the blowholes were certainly a worry in so far as small boys would be likely to become too inquisitive when in their vicinity, as well as being regarded as a hazard to the unsuspecting who could have walked that way in the dark.

In a moment of blinding inspiration Br James decided to cure all that and they became, for one glorious period of gay abandon, his new rubbish dump. What went down there apart from at least one ancient landrover there is no knowing. It is not the sort of thing of which an inventory would have been kept. But the blowholes are just about full now. And the long days of summer will pass, and the wild days of winter will come and go, until other springs and summers come and, with the passing years, nature will send seeds to grow and to hide the man-made scars. And, walking above and over them in safety, the readers of the secondary sources will search in vain. Br James will have been forgotten, and the blowholes shall be no more.

Before Dom James Wicksteed resigned he had already appointed Fr Robert O'Brien as Prior. In the situation in which the Community found themselves on Dom James' resignation, authority reverted to the mother house at Chimay, and the Abbot, Dom Guerric Baudet, appointed Fr Robert as Superior *ad nutum*. That is the position at the time of writing.

Fr Robert had at one time been in charge of the dairy and was conversant with what was happening on the farm when Fr David Luscombe-King left in 1975. Having been Prior for some time he had a comprehensive knowledge of the Community's business affairs and their secular needs. He has managed to borrow monks from other monasteries, but it will have to be some time before it can be known whether any of them will continue on loan for as long as Br James.

Recently, too, a Friends of Caldey group has come into being, with able-bodied well-wishers coming to the island for one or two weeks during the year to do some of the manual jobs which need doing. There are also the regular seasonal helpers who come every year to help in the tea-house and shops.

The result of all this is that over the last year or so there has been something happening and a new air of buoyancy has been discernible. What the future holds for any of us we cannot know, which is just as well. And things can change quite suddenly.

In the Caldey archives there is a letter from Dom Aelred Carlyle, written in 1951 when he was in Vancouver, to the Prior of Caldey. Dom Aelred referred to a letter he had recently received from Peter Anson who had said he did not think that Caldey would have room for the growing Novitiate unless the burnt-out cottages were rebuilt. The bright picture he would seem to have

Friends of Caldey stone walling, 1983

painted was in sharp contrast to the pessimistic views he expressed when he was quoted in a rather foolish feature in the *Western Mail* twenty years later. The article was typical and caused much resentment on the island. The reporter went over to talk to the Abbot, which he was given every facility to do, but met Peter Anson, who by that time seemed to have developed something of a death wish on the place, and angled the story on that. There was, of course, a measure of truth in what was said, but the gloomy forecasts were exaggerated out of all proportion to the true position.

A few years later H.T.V. screened a programme called 'They Came To An Island.' It was idiotic and laughable, but also quite disgraceful. They hired monks' habits from somewhere, dressed people up in them, and stuck them in a boat with their backs to the camera to make it look as if they were fishing off the island. The Abbot said in a memo:

> The producer infiltrated himself into the Guesthouse, and only subsequently revealed that he was a television producer gathering

material for a programme on the Island. In view of this behaviour, I refused to have anything to do with the project.

Later on H.T.V. asked for permission to make a short documentary film on fishing off the Island. I agreed to this after receiving an assurance from them that it had nothing whatever to do with the earlier project. There is no doubt in my mind, however, that this was the origin of the bogus monks fishing off the Island in the film.

So far as I am concerned H.T.V. are out since they do not observe the rules of civilised conduct.

It is perhaps rather hard on H.T.V. as a company to be judged on the behaviour of one particular person. Shades of J. C. Griffith Jones who, when he went to Caldey fifty years ago, represented himself as an archaeologist. When one rogue badger breaks into the hen-house the whole of an otherwise thoroughly decent species is given a bad name. It is well-known to every reasonable journalist who has ever been to Caldey, and behaved as properly as the vast majority of them do, that they are received with courtesy and kindness and afforded every help.

Whatever views are presented, however, and no matter how their fortunes may fluctuate, it is greatly to be hoped that the Community's future can be assured. It is not only for what they may achieve for mankind through their lives of devotion and prayer as monks on behalf of their fellow-men. There is also the question of what they do by providing for spiritual help and retreat.

In the first place, of course, there is the question of what they may have been able to do over the years for their own kind. There is, for example, a charming letter in the archives from a monk, Christophe de Bisschop of Mont des Cats, written to the Community during the war:

> I have known, by Rev. Fat. Abbot: Mulachie of Mount St Bernard Abbey, Coalville, Leicester, the adresse of your monastery: N.D. of Caldey, Tenby and of the convent: N.D. of Stapehill, Winborne Dorset of the O.C.R.
>
> I am one religious monk choirbrother of the monastery of Sancta Maria-de-monte O.C.R. situated to North of France—Mobilised soldier of the war, i've been wounded near Dunkirk and evacuated by

a british-ship in England, where i am into Stoke military hospital—Devonport the 3th June which is into the diocese of Plymouth, as well as your both communities. We are therefore very neighbours I shall soon been cured, because my wound is small and superficial, and i receive good cares from nurses skilful and devoted. As soon as i should been free, i shall like much to go at Dorset or Caldey, if it is possible. Will you, please, write to me if you can welcome me into your monastery sometime, meanwhile the lucky instant when i should can join again my natal nest: Sia Mia de Mt. Beforehand, i thanks many. Excuse the bad translation of this letter, because i do not know much the english language. Oremus pro pace, pro invicem and pro fratribus nostris absentibus. Jube, Domne Reverende Abbas, benedicere filium tuum religiosum ac devotum in X—to et M—ia

f.M. Christophe O.C.R.

To have received such a plea from a monk who found himself in a strange land in time of war is no more than would have been expected. But the readiness to receive those in need goes far, far beyond concern for their own kind. Nobody will ever know the extent of the indebtedness of the mentally and spiritually broken and lost, who have turned to Caldey in their need, or have been directed there by priests or ministers.

Nor is this all. Caldey has not merely become a haven for the lost. For a long time now the Community there, originally perhaps at the instigation of Dom James Wicksteed, have been giving a positive lead towards Christian unity and tolerance, and Fr Robert has continued where Dom Wicksteed left off. Not only are more and more groups, of all Christian denominations, going to Caldey for retreats but, where their limited resources permit, the Community try also to identify with other Christian fellowships in the area.

In our own chapel at Amroth, which is of the United Reformed Church, a little while ago, the service should have been taken by a Baptist minister. At the last minute he was unable to fulfil the commitment and he arranged for a friend of his, an Anglican, or Church in Wales, priest to come in his place. When, at a later date, the Baptist minister did come to us, he remarked how it was a refreshing sign of the times that such a thing could have happened. He then went on to say that only recently he and his fellow ministers of the various denominations in his town had just been giving a farewell party to the departing Roman Catholic priest. What is sad is that the position has arisen that such events should be worthy of comment.

Not all Catholic priests, of course, are out of this same good Christian mould, but the Caldey Community, at any rate, are doing what they can in the area of which, insular though they are, they have become a part. For nearly ten years Fr Robert has been taking the occasional service in our chapel, as have other members of the Community, and they have taken part in worship with other Christian fellowships in the area.

On all fronts, of course, enlightened Christians are working towards unity. I offered the thought in *Total Community* that Christians could not afford to dissipate their energies in arguing about those points on which they disagree, when there are so many issues on which they agree, in an age when the real enemy is the false god of materialism. Not only am I more convinced than ever that I was right in saying this, but I would now go further and say that, if we spend our time talking of the things on which we agree, then we are likely to find that there is not much time left to argue about those things on which we differ and that, come to think of it, they are not all that important anyway. Certainly, if we start off by trying to sort out the arguments of those things on which we differ, we just get bogged down right at the start and never get anywhere.

In any case, what are some of these supposedly great differences? I have heard Nonconformists complain about Catholics asking Saints to intercede for them. We tell people that we pray for them, and we do pray for them. We ask others to pray for us. As Christians we know that the grave is empty. We know that our loved ones we have lost for a while have only gone as far as God and that God is very near. And we know that God is in us, and grows and works in us, so what harm in asking those loved ones to pray for us now that they are perhaps a bit nearer to God than we are? If we could ask them to pray for us before, we can ask them now. So why not ask the Saints as well? I have no objection for I need all the help I can get.

And the best Saint of all, of course, just has to be the one whom God chose to be the Mother of His own Son. Could any ordinary mortal possibly honour her as much as God honoured her? So where does the idea come from that she can be honoured too much?

We live in an age when the family is the one sure bastion against the permissiveness of the pornographers, abortionists, drug pedlars and all the others who have laid siege to society. The Communists, who are without Christ, know exactly what they are doing when they break up the family. So maybe it is not such a bad idea for Christians to remember the importance of the Holy Family. It was hardly an easy decision for Mary to accept what God was asking for her. If it were to happen today the neighbours would say, 'That's a likely story,' and urge her to have an abortion.

God took human form in order to bring mankind back to Himself. By doing it in the way He did, with Mary's consent, did He not emphasise the importance He placed on family life?

As the Rev R. W. Connelly wrote in *Walsingham Is For Today*:

> All devotion is based on a proper understanding of Our Lady's role. She is the Mother of God and we honour her for that reason. Without her Son, she is just one of us; with her Son, she is the most important human creature of all time.
>
> As the Mother of Jesus, she shared his love as only a mother can share; she gave him human life that he might save the world; she interested herself in every detail of his mission; she followed him in suffering to the very foot of the Cross.
>
> It is the bond of love uniting Mother to Son and Son to Mother which is the basis of Catholic devotion. Because Christ, who is God, loves his Mother in this special way, he listens readily to her prayer and accords to her an extraordinary power of intercession. Because Mary loves her Son as Man and God, her love includes an unusual affection for God's children on earth. She ardently desires to use her power of intercession and to further Christ's mission on earth: The salvation and happiness of all men.
>
> Mary is an enigma. On the one hand so close to God; on the other hand so ordinary human. It is so easy to exaggerate her role until she seems to be indistinguishable from God himself; it is also easy to

minimize her role so that she appears to be an ordinary woman indistinguishable from the rest of the human race. To exaggerate or to minimize is not to honour.

The heart of the matter is Mary's relationship with God. As long as she is seen as the 'Christ bearer', the Mother of God, then she will be seen in her true perspective.

In the statue at Walsingham the Child seems to dominate with the Mother in the background. The Child holds the book of Gospels with one hand and with the other seems to shield his Mother from attack.

I referred earlier to the fact that there is now a statue of the Blessed Virgin in what was once the old pump-house in the village and that one of the village ladies always ensured that there were fresh flowers there. The village lady these days is Peter Cummins' wife, Joyce, and it is appropriate that she lives in No 5

Joyce Cummins renewing the flowers at the village shrine of Our Lady of Walsingham

cottage in the village, because it was in that cottage Mrs Charis Stanton lived who placed the statue there.

Mrs Stanton spent time on the island years ago as a girl in Done Bushell's time and came back to live there in the 1940s. In 1948 she went to Walsingham to represent Caldey in a national pilgrimage and wrote to ask her daughter, Caroline, who was living in London, to obtain for her a statue of Our Lady of Walsingham. Caroline had one made by a community of Anglican nuns. Mrs Stanton took it with her to Walsingham, where it was blessed, then brought it home to Caldey and had it placed in its present position, and always kept fresh flowers there. With the ecumenical trend developing at Walsingham it is fitting that this should be the statue at Caldey.

A while ago, when I was on a visit to Caldey, Fr Robert asked me if Ebenezer, our chapel at Amroth, would like a statue of the Blessed Virgin and Child. It was the last one to have been completed by Br Stanislaus, another dear soul, who will be remembered by those who did not have the privilege of knowing him, as the monk who died peacefully in the kitchen whilst making coffee for the rest of the Community at three o'clock in the morning. He used to make the statues for sale.

Without exception, every one of our members was delighted to accept. So then, as we had no minister at the time, I phoned our Moderator, Dr John Morgans. He has been leading parties on retreats to Caldey since 1971, when he was a minister at Llanidloes. He, too, thought the offer of the gift was splendid.

The previous year, he said, he had been at a conference of the World Council of Churches at Geneva and a prominent Nonconformist had offered the opinion from the platform that the time was long overdue for us to attach more importance to the Mother of Our Lord. And the Moderator added, as his own thought, that we should remember that it is the mothers who have handed down the Apostolic Faith to their children for generations.

I have no idea what anyone else may think about this, but I would say it denotes progress.

Dom Robert O'Brien with Dr John Morgans, Moderator U.R.C. (right) and
Dom Celsus, Abbott of Portlegnone   *Russel Davies*

Chapter 22

Bringing it up-to-date

I fear I have digressed slightly but, having made the point earlier that I was going to write my own book, maybe that will not upset the critics too much. And there are still some facts and figures to be recorded for the sake of posterity to bring the story up-to-date.

There are many factors which influence farming policies on any farm, and particularly is this so on an island. I discussed all this, both in *Total Community* and *The Sounds Between*, so there is no point in repeating it here where it must suffice to record merely what is happening at the moment.

History has shown that sheep farming has always been the basis of the economy on the Pembrokeshire islands whenever they have been farmed successfully, and I believe that that will continue to be true in the future. That is not to suggest that there

Sheep have always been an important part of the island economy, 1949

are not other enterprises which can, and must, have their proper place.

Back in the 1960s sheep were doing so badly that agricultural advisers on every side were saying there was no room for sheep and to get rid of them. The advisers based their opinions on economic considerations. As a breed, farmers are too wise to be greatly influenced by such talk. Now, of course, the wheel has turned and there are those who would say to double the number of sheep being kept, in the fond notion that twice as many would make twice as much money.

On Caldey there are now 130 breeding ewes, mostly speckle-faced, with two speckle-faced rams and two Suffolks. There is a well-worn farming adage that one sheep is another sheep's worst enemy. So, if the sheep flock on Caldey is to be doubled, who is going to go round in advance making good all the walls on a wind-swept island where no hedges grow? That is an interesting question which might just exercise the attention of the Friends of Caldey for some time to come. Successful sheep-farming depends absolutely in the first place on the ability to control the stock, and that calls for better fencing, or walling, than exists on Caldey at the moment. The Good Book also exhorts us to be moderate in all things.

Recently, that is at the end of May 1983, some lambs went to market from Caldey at sixty pounds liveweight and they made £40 apiece. I mention the fact purely as a matter for consideration by somebody or other a hundred years from now.

At this moment in time,—which is a horrible piece of jargon, meaning now, which has crept into our language of recent years, and which will no doubt be accepted as having been standard ancient usage by whoever is trying to work out the significance of sixty pounds liveweight at £40 apiece a hundred years hence,— there are two herds of cattle on Caldey. There is a dairy herd and a beef-suckler herd.

The Jersey herd consists of twenty-two milking cows plus a Jersey bull, and the heifers are reared for herd replacements. A spring-calving policy is followed, so that the bulk of the milk is available for the summer season. Sales of liquid milk away from the island are not possible so that, apart from milk consumed on the island, the remainder is used for the manufacture of butter, yoghurt, cream, ice cream, clotted cream and cheese-cakes.

At the moment there is a small pig enterprise consisting of three Large White sows and a boar. The progeny are fed on skim milk and barley and sold either as porkers or for bacon.

There are sixteen Charolais cross Hereford beef cows, and a bull of similar breeding is used for the production of single-suckled calves. These are fattened off hay and grass and are sold at either eleven or eighteen months of age. The size of the crate available for transport continues to be a limiting factor.

It is this question of transport to the mainland which has a significant bearing on all the farm enterprises. It is possible that one day serious consideration will again have to be given to the possibility of slaughtering on the island. It has been done before, so it could be done again. The only difference now is that there are more officials to be kept in gainful employment, more forms to be filled in and more, many more, bureaucratic regulations with which to comply.

An integral part of the farming programme is now the corn growing. With sheep to maintain the fertility, a hundred acres of corn are now being grown. Of this acreage, eighty acres are under oats and twenty under barley. Oats are not as demanding of lime as barley is and, with the day of the lime-kiln having passed long since, the transporting of lime for use on the land must always represent a major difficulty.

Hitherto there has been a heavy waste of straw, for transport has always militated against selling to the mainland. There was a classic example of this back in the mid-1970s during a season of exceptionally severe drought, when crops of grass and corn were so slight that hay and straw were making astronomical prices. The Community have for long been fully paid up members of the National Farmers Union and, thinking to be of some help, offered the surplus straw on Caldey to anyone who could arrange to fetch it. The local group secretary of the N.F.U. tried his best to get something organised, but there were no takers. It is one thing to cart straw across country to west Wales from East Anglia. It is another thing altogether to get it across a couple of miles of water in an open boat. If it does not make sense in seasons when straw is in such demand it demonstrates clearly the frustrations of those who would seek to farm an island successfully in normal times. A few hundred bales were sold to a local farmer during the winter, but that was done as a favour and was something of a headache for all concerned.

Now, however, the installation of a straw-burner has changed all that. It will, in fact, burn just about anything, including all the packing from the goods which come to the island shops. But last winter it burnt four thousand bales of straw from the farm and they were credited at fifty pence per bale in the farm accounts.

The monastery church is heated by electric storage heaters. They were installed in 1965 after the coming of the main supply. As the saying goes, it seemed like a good idea at the time. But, at today's electricity charges, the Community are very pleased that they did not also replace the central heating system in the monastery itself. About two thousand bales of straw are used for bedding purposes for the farm stock and the remainder can now be put to excellent use for heating the monastery.

This innovation has been accompanied by the installation also of a wood burning stove in the refectory. It burns wood from the island's fallen trees, and also driftwood, and heats water for the kitchen, scullery, bakery, one radiator and Bar-Jona. This is a little room adjoining the kitchen where they make and drink the occasional quick cup of coffee. The name derives, I believe, from Vatican II when convenient places were installed behind the pillars of St Peter's to which the bishops could repair for a quiet cup of tea. Bar-Jona was Simon Peter's other name. Not a bad pun, I think, even by monastic standards.

All this revision of heating methods has seen the end of the barbaric practice of having to unload coal boats into carts on the open beach. Sufficient has already been written on that subject for it to be unnecessary further to revive hideous memories for those still alive who suffered in the cause.

I suggested in *Total Community* that, on the farm, it looked as if the rabbit pest had been eliminated at last. Originally there was a

Unloading coal, 1923

By 1963 the horse and cart had been replaced

Unloading coal was always thirsty work—1950

1983   The mobile crane makes life easier but transport is still costly

spectacular crash in the rabbit population following the first outbreak of the disease myxomatosis in the county in 1954. In the absence of such predators as stoats, weasels and foxes, the rabbit numbers soon built up again to be followed by another outbreak of myxomatosis. This has been the recurring pattern on the other Pembrokeshire islands of Skomer and Ramsey. Following the last outbreak on Caldey in the early 1970s, the young farm manager at that time, Fergus Cummings, along with Br James, led a determined attempt to seek out and destroy the survivors and, by 1975, it looked as if the attempt had been successful. For every rabbit that is seen in the open there can be twenty or a hundred underground or in the undergrowth. It is idle to suppose, therefore, that, because no rabbits are seen, there are none about. After a further eight years, however, it can now be said with confidence that there are no longer rabbits on Caldey.

The benefit of being without these pests is incalculable. Few people would begrudge rabbits the little they eat. The real charge against them is the damage they do.

When rabbits were still a problem, 1948

If anyone doubts this they need only take a look at what is happening on Ramsey. I have just referred to recurring outbreaks of myxomatosis. The point is that with each recurrence of any disease it becomes attenuated. It is in fact believed, for example, that the common cold of today is an attenuation of the Great Plague of the 17th century. Myxomatosis has now become so attenuated on Ramsey that it is no longer a feasible solution to the problem there. And problem it certainly is. John Freeman and his wife, Alison, are making a courageous attempt to wrest a living from the island against all the odds, but the place is overrun with rabbits, and the solution to this problem is only one of those on which their whole future depends. Times have changed considerably since the days of long ago when rabbits on the islands were a source of income.

There is no record of any shooting on Caldey in days gone by, apart from the indiscriminate shooting of the sea-birds, and such occasional references as we have to the shooting of wild-duck. Aelred Carlyle's pheasants, however, continued to breed on the island. Permission had been given for various people to shoot from time to time and, after the senseless manner of the occasional irresponsible individual, the last pheasants were shot. Fergus, with a great interest in country things, introduced some more pheasants, and a couple of local boys have also put down some young birds and sent over sittings of pheasant's eggs. This is just for the joy of seeing pheasants about the place, and a great joy it is to be sure, both to see them and to hear their call.

I mentioned earlier the fact that, in spite of the persistent taking of gulls' eggs over the years, these birds had continued to increase until recently. The Act passed to protect the sea-birds failed to do so because of the side-effect of the internal combustion engine and the steady discharge of waste oil at sea. The taking of their eggs for centuries had had no effect. Whilst the auks declined steadily in numbers the gulls increased. Local naturalist, Stephen Sutcliffe, carried out a count in 1970 and reckoned there were 2,500 breeding pairs of gulls on Caldey. In 1975 the figure was 3,300. In 1978 it had dropped to 2,350 and, by 1982, the number was down to 887 pairs.

True, Tenby's direct outfall sewerage scheme was replaced by a treatment works, thus removing one of the sources of food for the gulls, but not enough to account for such figures. In any case, the same thing has been happening elsewhere in South Wales all along the Bristol Channel. Current thinking is that the sudden decline is directly related to the introduction of black plastic bags by local authorities in 1974 for collecting of refuse. These bags are believed to create the warm conditions conducive to the breeding of the bacillus *botulinus*. It is known that the gulls tend to feed at refuse tips as the rubbish is delivered, and many have been dying of botulinum poisoning since that time. The Americans call it 'duck disease'.

The decline in the gull population is no bad thing. They are scavengers by nature and come to the islands only to breed. In excessive numbers they become predators and are notorious thieves of the eggs and young of the sea-birds which nest upon the ledges. Whether these auks are likely to show any increase in numbers now that the gulls have declined it is difficult to say, for they have so many other factors stacked against them.

Members of the Flat Earth Society will no doubt demand a cessation of the age-old custom of taking the gulls' eggs, but I hope no one will suggest that members of the Flat Earth Society should also be exterminated. They do not do as much damage as the rabbits or gulls and are really rather harmless.

There is one other aspect of the island's wild life which should be touched on for the sake of the record, although it is now becoming ancient history. In the 1950s the then chairman of what was at that time the West Wales Field Society put some Soay sheep on St Margaret's. It was a slip-shod, badly run organisation. In 1959 there were some stormy meetings and the allegations made at them can all be read in local papers of the time. Eventually members were able to remove the chairman and, at a later date, the secretary. Now, as the West Wales Naturalists' Trust, it does a useful job of work.

One of the criticisms was that the Soay sheep on St Margaret's had been left to die in the drought of 1959 and that the chairman, who also had the grandiose title of honorary warden, had done nothing about it, although he had been told of their plight. At the meeting when the matter was considered, the chairman reported that the sheep had been struck by lightning and, by a narrow majority, members voted to accept this report. Br James, however, had been carrying out some of his archaeological digging in the vicinity of Eel Point at the time and was able to tell of the true position. I would not like any of the quoters of secondary sources to confine themselves to the chairman's report for that year when much other information is readily available. Apart from any other considerations, anyone who has ever seen Soay sheep in action will know that lightning could never catch them.

Lastly, there must be a word on the bees. For some years, until recently, Fr Anselm Simpson was the monastery's apiarist. When age began to take its toll there was no one for a time who could take on the job. Then there came to the island as a helper, Miss Rita Cunningham, an ex-Carmelite nun, who can and does turn

Rita Cunningham

her hand to just about anything. And it transpired that she had had much experience with bees. So Rita has become the new apiarist, what remained of the bee population has been moved from the gorse bushes in, what was for her, the forbidden territory in the monastic enclosure above Paul Jones Bay, and she has now set up bee hives in the area of the old gardens, up by the Priory, with an importation of bees of the famous strain from Buckfast Abbey.

Again for the record, the farm staff, in addition to those already mentioned, is completed by Tenby-born Gwyn Bolton, known to the world in general as Blackie and who insists that the world in general must also know that he is not any sort of manager but a farm labourer and please to make that quite clear.

Former cigarette firm representative, David Philippart, is in charge of the dairy, and John Cattini, who married a niece of Br Thomas, is the manager in charge of the monks' commercial

Peter Cummins, Dave Philippart, Stephen Cummins and Gwyn Bolton

enterprises, including the two mainland shops in Tenby and Saundersfoot.

Patrick Kirkham is the monastery cook, and Tom Bassing-thwaighte is the chemist in the perfumery. When Josh Richards died, Clive Nation moved over to Caldey with his family, already having been working there for some time, and is now the man on general maintenance.

All this means that there are children on the island, and Audrey Robinson, the schoolmistress, has seven pupils in her care.

These days one of the monks acts as postmaster and, for the interest of the philatelists, since 1973 a stamp known as a Tenby 'Dab' has been available for an extra couple of pence. It has no valid use, but is something more than a novelty in so far as the money from the sales goes some way towards meeting the cost of running the island boat.

Apart from the employment of two men and a part-timer all the year round, boats have to be replaced. The present boat, *Caldey Abbey II*, cost £35,000, and there is also a second boat, the *Isle of*

Audrey Robinson and the Caldey school-children, 1983

Fr Stephen, Procurator, (2nd from right) meets the boatmen of the Tenby Pool
before the start of the summer season, 1983

Caldey. The crane on the jetty has now been replaced by a mobile
crane which cost £15,000.

Both boats participate in the well-established Tenby Pool and,
under the guidance of quiet-spoken Fr Stephen, the Island Procurator, this system continues to work well. It is traditional to make
jokes about the meanness of the Tenby boatmen, but I can only
say for my own part that I have never received anything but help
and every kindness from them. (Having said this I hope that at
least one of them might be persuaded to buy a copy of the book
when it appears, even if he charges the others for the loan of it.)

Also on the island one of the old army 'ducks' (DKW) is maintained for off-loading day-visitors in the peak of the season when
the low tide is out beyond the jetty.

There are those who will point to such expensive items as the
new boat and the crane to illustrate how much the monks must be

making, without seeming to understand that this is the sort of
money which has to be found to enable them to remain in
business. It is the sort of senseless talk with which farmers are only
too familiar whenever they have to buy a new tractor. And the
monks also need to do that from time to time, too.

There is an odd assortment of second-hand cars, vans and pick-
ups to be avoided as they wheeze round the island. Contrary to
popular belief they do not run on the power of prayer, although
anyone could be forgiven for thinking so, and petrol is brought
across in cans. Diesel fuel for the farm comes in drums.

The cost of all this can be imagined, and it means that any
building work, by the time the materials have been delivered,
costs about twice as much as it would on the mainland. Two new
shops have been built in recent years, one in place of the old
village hall. An extension is needed for the perfumery, and plans
are under consideration for a new school. All these things have to
be budgeted for.

It will be interesting to know what the story will be a hundred
years from now. And also, maybe, how the costs will strike whoever is sufficiently interested to read of them.

Mention of shops should not lead to the idea that they are shops
for the benefit of the islanders. They are merely shops where the
monks sell their own produce and souvenirs to the thousands of
visitors to the island during the season.

The islanders themselves rely on the mainland for their household needs, apart from milk and bread which are supplied by the
monastery. Weather permitting the boat, which is based at
Tenby, goes over every week-day in the winter with the post,
goods and anyone who has business on the island. About once a
week there will be two boats. This enables islanders to come over
to Tenby to shop and then return on the second boat. Every now
and again, according to the state of the tide, there is what is
known as a 'long boat'.

This is not something to do with any re-enactment of the
Vikings' way of life. It is simply that the first boat is early in the
morning and the second boat is late in the afternoon. So there is a
long time between each boat and this gives time for the islanders

to go a little further afield to do their shopping, maybe as far as Kilgetty to the Co-op, or even Carmarthen or Haverfordwest to Tesco and the great fashion houses. Some of them have their own cars on the mainland.

Way back in George Owen's time, it will be recalled, there was mention of the fact that, 'It is now grown a question in what hundred of Pembrokeshire this island should be . . . and inhabitants are content to rest exempt from any payments or taxations with any hundred . . .'

Since Owen's time not only have 'hundreds' disappeared from our way of rural administration, but, according to the bureaucrats, who arrived with the foisting of the monster known as Dyfed on an unsuspecting and ungrateful nation by Messrs Heath and Walker, Pembrokeshire has disappeared also. The time therefore seemed apposite for councillors to raise once again the question of Caldey's extra-parochial status, and committees were instructed to look into it.

One definition of a committee is that it is a body of the unfit appointed by the unwilling to do the unnecessary. An even better definition, particularly in this case, is that they sit down to do nothing and come to the conclusion that nothing can be done.

For a couple of years recently Caldey has been on the agenda of local government's discussions but, many miles of travelling expenses later, it has been decided that nothing can be done.

Maybe they were anxious that George Owen should not have to be re-written and nothing has been done to disturb the *status quo*.

So that just about completes the facts of the Caldey story as far as I have been able to discover and assess them. If it is too much to hope that I have not made any mistakes I hope I have not made too many. The truth of what I said at the beginning should now be abundantly clear. That is that there have been enough stories about Caldey over the years to provide material for quite a few more books. It is only when this one is published that people from all over the place will say, 'I wish I'd known you were writing a book and I could have told you about so-and-so, and there's a pity you didn't mention such-and-such'.

I have written nothing about the fact that the islanders pay no rates, receive no municipal services, and have no municipal vote, because it has all been written about before. So much of this, and more like it, can be found elsewhere, but I have told something of the Caldey story as I know it and have tried to establish it. It may well be that in a hundred, two hundred and more years from now, there will be those who will ask what manner of people were those who lived and moved and had their being on this island.

I trust I am not presuming too much in hoping that these pages will prove to be of some use to them, whilst recognising their many deficiencies and being fully conscious of the fact that material must exist for another ten or a dozen people to write their own versions.

I hope I may be spared long enough to read some of them.

More of a personal note

On January 6th, 1979 the Caldey Community celebrated the Golden Jubilee of their foundation. Only months previously two stalwart founder members of the Community, Fr Pascal and Fr Dominic, celebrated their Jubilees as ordained priests. Fr Herman was looking forward to celebrating his in the March of that year.

Fr Pascal, of whom it was said that he wrote poetry in English with a French accent, celebrated by writing a poem for the occasion. Fr Dominic asked that they might all have a glass of wine with their dinner.

The Cistercian newsletter for the Region of the Isles celebrated with a special Caldey Jubilee Issue. President of the Region, Dom Colmcille O'Toole, sent his greetings and, amongst other things, said, 'We say to the monks of Caldey on this occasion: thank you for being there, thank you for your rugged tenacity, thank you for the holiness which radiates from your island Abbey'.

In his report Fr Robert told something of the occasion. He wrote:

By Christmas, in spite of rough seas and an ailing boat and crane our renovation of the Church was completed by the erection of the new High Altar. It stands four square in two massive blocks of Portland stone. We have also foreshortened the Choir to allow the laity to participate more fully in our liturgy while preserving our enclosure. As the day approached the rough weather again seemed to threaten us . . . with a celebration even more homespun than we had envisaged. January 3rd . . . no boat, January 4th . . . no boat. Miraculously the wind died away and a great calm ensued. On January 5th our diocesan Bishop, Bishop Fox arrived and Fr Robert came as Dom Guerric's delegate from Scourmont. January 6th saw the homecoming of Bishop Gran from Oslo. At the concelebration the two Bishops presided and consecrated the new altar. The rite is a simple one these days compared with yesteryear's but it had lost nothing of its meaning and it was movingly carried out by Bishop Fox. Many of the islanders had come to the Mass with a few specially invited friends from Tenby and Swansea. All who could, came to the

Mgr John Gran, one time Caldey monk who became Bishop of Norway
(see *Total Community*)

buffet lunch and a merry time was had by all . . . till the fall of the tide necessitated the return of the travellers.

The report does not say so but, on the mainland, it was a time of bitterly cold winds, snow and hard frosts. It was only by a miracle that it was possible for friends to visit the island that day.

January 6th that year was a Saturday, and I remember it well. For Fr Robert referred to 'a few specially invited friends'. I did then, and always shall, count it as a great privilege that my wife and I were amongst the number. We were the only non-Catholics.

I shall never forget how happy she was that day, full of bright laughter and always happy to be involved. It was an understatement when Fr Robert reported that a merry time was had by all. When it came time to depart, my wife went with Zed, driving like Jehu, in a clapped-out shooting-brake, and Dom James Wicksteed and Bishop Fox as his other passengers, heading for the jetty and with a fair measure of hilarity. I walked. Not in any way showing off, but because there was no room for anybody else. Unlike Pyro of old, nobody fell in the water.

We returned home to the problem of frozen taps, burst pipes and treacherous roads.

It was one of our last outings together for, not long afterwards, I found her dead on the floor of the kitchen, one day as the light was fading, half-an-hour after leaving her in apparently good health.

Lucie her name was and, apart from the shock, after more than thirty-five years of partnership, the world was suddenly a different and rather lonely place. Readers who have travelled the same road will know what it is all about. When I met her I knew in ten seconds flat that that was it. Six weeks we spent in each other's company from the day we met until the day we married. In Aston parish church. Opposite the Villa ground. And me a rugby man.

There are those who say that talk of love at first sight is silly talk, but don't listen to them.

'Where both deliberate their love is slight,
Who ever loved that loved not at first sight?'

When it happens, it happens. That is not to say that life is all a bed of roses from there on. It is something that has to be worked at and cultivated. That is something I have always believed. And after more than thirty-five years I had no reason to change my mind.

Fr Robert came across for the funeral. The Abbot was a little concerned in case it should set a precedent, but said it had to be done. And Fr Robert gave the address at her funeral and, in our little chapel, with many more having to remain outside than could ever gain admission, paid eloquent tribute to a wonderful person of marvellous Christian qualities.

The Rev Emrys Davies, one time U.R.C. minister at Tenby, who was also our overseeing minister at Amroth, before we had a group minister, and who was a good friend of Caldey, wrote to me. I had, literally, some hundreds of letters at that time, because Lucie had been so universally well loved. Not least were the many messages from Caldey and a dear, dear nun, Sr Imelda, from Llandovery.

If people ever want to talk about the waste when men and women become monks or nuns, don't let them waste their time by trying to tell me. They were all a marvellous comfort.

But it was something which Emrys wrote which left a deep impression on me—'May you have faith and hope to live now one day at a time—just one day, and start again from there, accepting and adjusting. Expect the unexpected and the surprising. It is the way God works.'

When the gulls were nesting in the spring it seemed to be a good idea to go to Caldey and make my small contribution towards controlling them. For some years I had been doing it. But this time Lucie would not be with me and there was a temptation to run away. Even so, I went.

I referred earlier to Lizzie James, daughter of Henry James, engineman, who left Caldey and married and thereby became Lizzie Griffiths. She had one daughter, Margaret, who was head of the infants' school in Tenby. For various reasons, when our son started school, it was to Margaret Griffiths' school he went, and a good thing it proved to be. She married in due season and, since she married a man by the name of Tom James, she became

Margaret James. So there we are back with a James of Caldey again.

(I did say, did I not, that this was going to be my own book?)

Of course, Margaret James has nothing to do with the personal nature of this chapter, but I mention her just for the sake of causing a little more confusion.

I went to Caldey that week-end and, the day I arrived, met a girl, a nurse from Swindon, by the name of Margaret James. It turned out that she had gone there because she, too, had problems. She was a Catholic, but that was not one of her problems. And if she wants to write of her own problems she must do it for herself instead of just typing this.

I met her at eleven o'clock in the morning and made a date to go picking gulls' eggs at two o'clock that afternoon. By the lily-pond, down by the village green, I met her, took one look and said to myself that's it.

Walking by the blowholes, before Br James had filled them in, I explained to her about the mortal danger and suggested she should take my hand. There was probably the distance of a cricket pitch between them, but so what.

At four o'clock that same afternoon I asked her to marry me and she said (I have never allowed her to forget it) 'It's rather sudden'.

But having a cup of coffee in the lounge of the monastery's guest rooms the following morning, she said, 'I can see the sort of man you are. You won't give me any peace until I agree to marry you.'

I said, 'That's right.'

'All right,' she said, 'I'll marry you.'

With her sound Catholic thinking she said later, 'Nobody's going to marry us. We shall be marrying each other.'

And that is what we did, in our chapel at Amroth, with Fr Robert and my own minister, the Rev Hugh St John Gray, as witnesses, or conducting the service, or whatever it is would be the proper expression.

And, through the chapel window, in the autumn sunshine, Caldey could be seen across the bay.

Bibliography

Ch. 1

C.A.   Bushell, W. Done, *Caldey: An Island of the Saints*, 1908.

P.C.L.   Hoare, Geoffrey G., *Caldey: An Isle of the Severn Sea*, 1936.

P.C.L.   Daniel, Catherine, *Bardsey, Gate of Heaven*.

T.M.   *Royal Commission's Inventory of Ancient Monuments on Pembrokeshire*, 1925.

Howells, R., *Total Community*, 1975.

Howells, R., *The Sounds Between*, 1968.

C.A.   *Requisition on Title*, 1894.

Total Community, p. 184.

P.C.R.   *Tenby Church Register*

P.C.R.   *Census Returns*, 1881.

Howells, R., *Old Saundersfoot*, 1977, pp. 113-114.

Ch. 2

The Sounds Between, 2nd Edtn, 1976.

Hepper, F. N., *Flora of Caldey Island*, *(Proceedings of the Botanical Society of the British Isles)*, 1954.

Wintle, James, *The Coasts of Caldey*, 1922.

C.A.   *Pax*, Vol. 65, Sept. 1922.

Pax, 1924.

Caldey: An Isle of the Severn Sea.

T.M.   *Tenby Observer*, 1867.

T.M.   *Mason's Illustrated Guide to Tenby*, 1870.

The Benedictines of Caldey Island, 1912.

Gwynne, Fanny Price, *Sketches of Tenby and its Neighbourhood*, 1852.

P.C.L.   Mathew, Murray A., *The Birds of Pembrokeshire and its Islands*, 1894.

O'Neill, R. J. de C., *A Modern Pilgrimage*, 1931.

Royal Commission's Inventory of Ancient Monuments on Pembrokeshire, 1925.

T.M.   Leach, A. L., *Tenby and County News*, 1925.

Ch. 3

Lacaille, A. D. and Grimes, W. F., *Archaeologia Cambrensis*, Part I, 1955; Part II, 1961.

Leach, A. L., *Pax*, 1917.

Van Nedervelde, Br. James; Davies, M.; John, B. S., *Nature in Wales*, Vol. 245, Oct. 1973.

Howells, R., *Tenby Old and New*, 1981.

Bowen, E. G., *The Settlements of the Celtic Saints*, 1954.

C.A.   *Letter from Mrs. Dorothy Lyon, 8 Librarium Personnal*.

Cowley, F. G., Personal correspondence.

Macalister, R. A. S., *Corpus Inscriptionum Insularum Celticorum*, 1945, Vol. I.

Pritchard, Emily, *The History of St. Dogmael's Abbey*, 1907.
Cistercian Community, *Isle of Caldey*, 1931.
Lloyd, John Edward, *A History of Wales*, 1912.
Total Community, p. 22.
The Sounds Between, 2nd Edtn., p. 168.
Ibid, p. 49.
Bardsey, Gate of Heaven.
Caldey: An Isle of the Severn Sea.
P.C.R.   Wormoll, R. H., *Field Notes on Tenby*, 1937-8.
Roch, Fflorens, *The Isle of Caldey.*
Hirsch-Davies, J. E. De, *Catholicism in Wales*, 1915.

Ch. 4

Caldey: An Island of the Saints.
Caldey: An Isle of the Severn Sea.
The Sounds Between, p. 168.
Pax, No. 72, 1924.
Charles, B. G., *Old Norse relations with Wales*, 1934.
Ibid, *Non-Celtic place-names in Wales*, 1938, and personal correspond-
    ence.
The History of St. Dogmael's Abbey.
Bremer, *Works of Giraldus Cambrensis*, Vol. I.
Charles, B. G., Personal note.
The Sounds Between, p. 53.
P.C.L.   Owen, H., *Calendar of the Public Records relating to Pembrokeshire.*
N.L.W.   *Patent Rolls*, 1306-462.
N.L.W.   *Patent Rolls*, 1 Edw. 3, 1327, Jan. 30.
P.R.O.   *Patent Rolls*, Edward III (C66/166m m. 1).
The Sounds Between.
Howells, R., *Cliffs of Freedom*, 1961.
Leland, J., *The Itinerary in Wales*, 1536-9.
Itineraria Symonis Simeonis et Willelmi de Woodcestre, (James Nasmith,
    Ed., 1778).

Ch. 5

Knowles & Hadcock, *Mediaevl Religious Houses in England and Wales*,
    1953.
The History of St. Dogmaels's Abbey.
N.L.W.   Episcopal Register of St. David's, Vol. II, 1407-1518.
Williams, Glanmor, *The Welsh Church—From Conquest to Reformation*,
    1976.
P.R.O.   Ministers' Accounts, No. 5287, 27-8, Henry VIII.
Owen, George, *Elizabethan Pembrokeshire*, Ed., Brian Howells, 1973.
The History of St. Dogmael's Abbey.
P.C.R.   Jones, Francis, *Notes on Caldey*, 1965.

P.C.L.   Green, Francis, *West Wales Historical Records*, Vol. 5, p. 234.
Ibid., Vol. 24, p. 58.
Ibid., Vol. 24-21, Eliz. Sept. 14th (1579) No. 41.

Ch. 6

Laws, Edward & Edwards, Emily Hewlett, *Church Book of St. Mary, the Virgin, Tenby*, 1907.
Pax, Vol. VIII, No. 49, Autumn 1916.
Elizabethan Pembrokeshire.
Pax, No. 89, Winter 1928.
B.M.   Add MSS 22623, f27B.
The Sounds Between, p. 65.
Green, Francis, Vol. 12, p. 262.
Green, Francis, Vol. 12, p. 135 (Patent Rolls).
Elizabethan Pembrokeshire.
Fenton, R., *A Historical Tour through Pembrokeshire*, 1811.
The Sounds Between, p. 65.

Ch. 7

Treble, J., *Tenby. An Historical Sketch of the Place*, 1818.
N.L.W.   *Eaton Evans and Williams Papers*, 254 of Group I.
T.M.   *Select Remains of the Learned John Ray*, MDCCLX.
Green, Francis, Vol. 14, p. 201 *(Wills at Carmarthen).*
Treasury Papers, 1708-14, Vol. 113, f6.
Green, Francis, Vol. 13, p. 266 *(State Papers*—Vol. 4, p. 102).
The Sounds Between.
N.L.W.   Morris, L., *Plans of Harbours*, 1748.
N.L.W.   *Eaton Evans and Williams Papers*, No. 253 of Group I.
N.L.W.   Banks, S. S., Journal of an Excursion to Wales, 1767—Ms. 147C.
N.L.W.   Notebook of *A Journey to Tenby*, 1787. Ms. 9352A.
P.C.R.   Lease between Rev. John Henry Williams and John Loveday.
Caldey: An Isle of the Severn Sea.
Pax, No. 76. Autumn 1925.
C.A.   *Agreement between David Llewhellin and Thomas Kynaston*, 1798.
N.L.W.   *Williams & Williams Deeds, Haverfordwest*, 13881.

Ch. 8

Pax, No. 69, Winter 1923.
Leach, A. L., *Tenby and County News*, Dec. 31st, 1942.
Caldey: An Island of the Saints.
A Historical Tour through Pembrokeshire.
Old Saundersfoot.
C.A.   Map of 1897 *Schedule.*
The Coasts of Caldey.
Transactions Carmarthen Antiquarian Society, XII, 43, ill.

Miss Bridie Cummins, Personal Information.
Rt. Rev. Dom Robert O'Brien, Personal Information.
Cistercian Community, *Caldey Island, Dyfed.*
Report of the Commissioners of Inquiry into the state of Education in Wales,
    1847. Part I, Appendix, p. 475.
Bourne, Mary Anne, *A Guide to Tenby and its Neighbourhood,* 1843.
Tenby Observer, June 15th, 1855.
Venn, J. A., *Alumni Cantabrigienses,* Part II (1752-1900), 1947.
Crockford's Clerical Directory, 1860.
Archaeoligia Cambrensis, 1870, IV 1, 124 ill.
Ibid, 1855, 3rd Series, No. IV.
Sketches of Tenby and its Neighbourhood.
Harries, D. C., *Caldey, Monastery Isle,* 1956.
P.C.R.   *Penally Church Registers.*
P.C.R.   *Census Returns,* 1841, '51, '71.
Cambrian Journal, 1854.
Timmins, H. Thornhill, *Nooks and Corners of Pembrokeshire,* 1895.
A Historical Tour through Pembrokeshire.
Select Remains of the Learned John Ray.
Rees, W., *South Wales and the Border in the Fourteenth Century,*
    Ordnance Survey, 1933.
Tenby Observer, Oct. 19th, 1855.
Ibid, Jan. 2nd, 1868.
Catholic Directory of Saints.
Attwater, D., *The Penguin Dictionary of Saints,* 1965.
Butler, *Lives of the Saints.*
Williams, David H., *Welsh Cistercians,* 1984.

Ch. 9

Donovan, *Excursions Through South Wales,* 1804.
Rees, William, *Beauties of Wales,* 1815.
P.C.R.   *Tenby and Penally Church Registers.*
N.L.W.   Cullum, Rev. Sir Thomas, *Diary of a Journey into South Wales,* 1811.
    MS5446 C.
C.R.O.   *John Francis Papers* (Peniel), Box 85.
N.L.W.   *Williams and Williams Deeds,* Vol. 3, 22716/7/8/9—1789.
Jenkins, J. Geraint, *Maritime Heritage,* 1982.
C.A.   *Schedule,* 1799.
P.C.R.   *Census Returns,* 1841, '51, '71, '81.
P.C.R.   Haverfordwest Gaol Register, PQ/AG/6.
Williams, David, *The Rebecca Riots,* 1955.
P.C.R.   Manorbier Church Register.
G.R.O.   Death Certificate, 9212 B; DX284391.
Mr. Spencer Herapath, personal correspondence.
Caldey: An Island of the Saints.

Ch. 10

Report of Commission of Inquiry into the state of Education in Wales,
   1847.
The Welshman, Jan. 2 and Jan. 9, 1835.
Leach, A. L., *Guide to Tenby,* 1898.
P.C.R.   *Census Returns,* 1841, '51, '71, '81.
A Guide to Tenby and its Neighbourhood.

Ch. 11

A Guide to Tenby and its Neighbourhood.
Pax, No. 59, May 1920.
Sketches of Tenby and its Neighbourhood.
Mason, R., *Tales and Traditions of Tenby,* 1858.
Potters Electric News, June 5th, 1861.
The Birds of Pembrokeshire and its Islands.
Cliffs of Freedom.
The Sounds Between.
Hall, Mr. & Mrs. S. C., *Tenby: Its History, Antiquities, Scenery,*
   Traditions and Customs, 1861.
Tenby Old and New.
Report of the Commission of Inquiry into the state of Education in Wales,
   1847.
Pembrokeshire Herald, March 18th, 1859.
G.R.O.   Marriage Certificate, 9191B; MB 290213.
J. H. Newman: Letters and Diaries, Vol. XI, Thos. Nelson, 1961.
Potters Electric News, Jan. 2nd, 1867.
C.A.   *Conveyance,* Nov. 25th, 1867.
Way, Albert, *Archaeologia Cambrensis,* 1870.
Pembrokeshire Herald, Jan. 28th, 1876.
T.M.   Leach, A. L., *Tenby and County News,* 1941.
T.M.   Letter from Hugh L. Bridger, unclassified.
P.C.R.   *R. Howells Collection,* HDX/93.

Ch. 12

Verney, Margaret M., *Lieut-Colonel John P. V. Hawksley, D.S.O.,*
   R.F.A., 1917.
Caldey: An Island of the Saints.
P.C.R.   *Census Returns,* 1871, '81.
P.C.R.   *Tenby Church Registers.*
Tenby Observer, Aug. 6th, 1891.
Jefferies, Richard, *Hodge and His Masters,* 1880.
C.A.   *Mortgage,* May 30th, 1876.
C.R.O.   *John Francis Papers.*
Miss Eira M. King, personal correspondence.
C.A.   *Conveyance,* April 3rd, 1894.

Ch. 13

William Done Bushell of Harrow, 1919.

C.R.O   *John Francis Papers.*

Pembrokeshire Herald, Jan. 20th, 1894.

Nooks and Corners of Pembrokeshire.

Pax, Vol. 8, No. 47, Spring 1916.

P.C.R.   *Census Returns.*

P.C.R.   *Tenby and Penally Church Records.*

Ch. 14

Anson, Peter F., *Abbot Extraordinary*, 1958.

William Done Bushell of Harrow.

C.R.O.   *John Francis Papers.*

C.A.   *Mortgage*, June 24th, 1899.

Letter in possession of Mrs. Margaret James.

C.A.   *Notes.*

The Sounds Between, 2nd Edtn., 1976.

Pax, No. 64, Sept. 1922.

Mr. Ivor John, personal conversation.

Mr. Haydn Williams, personal conversation.

Ch. 15

Miss Renée Haynes, personal correspondence.

C.R.O.   *John Francis Papers.*

Mr. Stuart Thomas, personal conversation.

Mr. Wynford Mabe, personal conversation.

Pax, No. 52, Autumn, 1917.

Pax, No. 37, Michaelmas, 1913.

Programmes in possession of Mrs. Margaret James.

Letter in possession of Mrs. Joy Davies.

Pax, No. 41, Michaelmas 1914.

Pax, No. 44, Summer 1915.

Ch. 16

Prinknash Abbey Archives, correspondence with Dom Hildebrand.

Mr. Bertie Hughes, personal conversation.

Pax, No. 48, Summer 1916.

Dom Michael Hanbury, personal conversation.

Pax, No. 42, Dec. 1914.

Pax, No. 87, Summer, 1928.

Total Community.

Pax, No. 47, Spring 1916.

Pax, Nos. 55-57, 1919.

Mr. Ivor John, personal conversation.

Pax, No. 58, Jan. 1920.

Miss Bridie Cummins, personal conversation.
Mrs. Cecilia Kilbride, personal conversation.
C.A. *Estate Papers.*

Ch. 17

Prinknash Abbey Archives, correspondence with Dom Hildebrand.
Mr. Ivor John, personal conversation.
Total Community.
The Sounds Between.
Pax, No. 72, Autumn 1924.
C.A. Notes on lease.
Pax, No. 72, Autumn 1924.
Ibid, No. 350, Summer 1982.
Ibid, No. 89, Winter 1928.
Tenby Observer, Jan. 18th, 1929.
Ibid, May 31st, 1929.
Ibid, July 26th, 1929.
C.A. Notes on lease.
The Penguin Dictionary of Saints.
C.A. *The Caldey Gossiper*, 1931.
Caldey: An Isle of the Severn Sea.

Ch. 18

Hodge and his Masters.
Pax, No. 56, Spring 1919.
P.C.R. *Census Returns*, 1881.
Pax, No. 7, Summer 1924.
P.C.R. *Tenby Church Registers.*
Pax, No. 56, Spring 1919.
Ibid, No. 84, Autumn 1927.
Mr. Stanley Thomas, personal conversation.
Total Community.

Ch. 19

Total Community.
C.A. Fr. Dominic's pictures.
C.A. Notes
Mr. Josh Richards, personal conversation.
C.A. Letters.
C.A. Personal notes.
Catholic Times, July 1905.

Ch. 20

Narberth Weekly News, March 8th, 1928.
Benedictines of Caldey, 1912.
Pax, No. 60, Nov. 1920.

Ch. 21

Total Community.
The Sounds Between.
C.A.   Letters.
            Western Mail, Nov. 27th, 1971.
C.A.   Memo.
            Connelly, R. W., *Walsingham is for today,* 1972.
            Miss Caroline Stanton, personal conversation.
            Dr. John Morgans, personal conversation.

Ch. 22

Total Community.
The Sounds Between.
Sutcliffe, S. J., *Gull Population in West Wales,* 1983.
Cliffs of Freedom, p. 148.
West Wales Guardian, April 17th and July 31st, 1959, and June 17th, 1960.
Western Telegraph, April 16th and July 30th, 1959, and June 16th, 1960.
Lockley, R. M., *Nature in Wales,* Vol. 6, Nos. 2 & 3.
Western Telegraph, April 29th, 1976.
Elizabethan Pembrokeshire.

Ch. 23

Region of the Isles, Cistercian Newsletter, 1979.

Abbreviations:

C.A.   Caldey Archives.
P.C.L.   Pembrokeshire County Library.
T.M.   Tenby Museum.
P.C.R.   Pembrokeshire County Records.
N.L.W.   National Library of Wales.
P.R.O.   Public Record Office.
B.M.   British Museum.
C.R.O.   Carmarthen Records Office.
G.R.O.   General Register Office.

Index

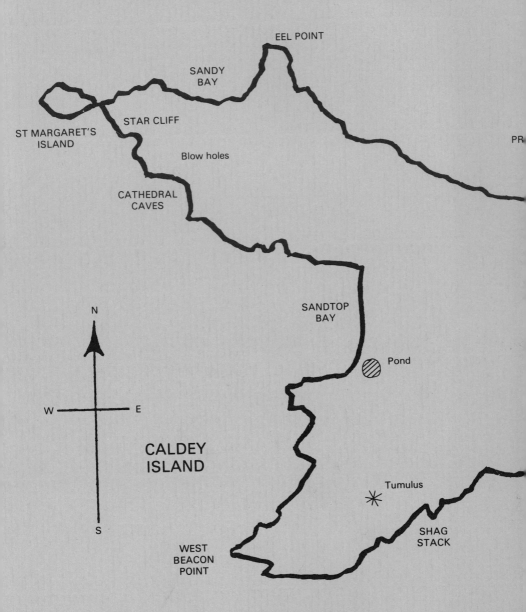

EEL POINT

SANDY
BAY

ST MARGARET'S
ISLAND

STAR CLIFF

Blow holes

CATHEDRAL
CAVES

PR

N

W —— E

S

CALDEY
ISLAND

SANDTOP
BAY

Pond

Tumulus

WEST
BEACON
POINT

SHAG
STACK

Large shaded portion — Monastic Enclosu